SHAKEN FOUNDATIONS

A Resource for Young Adults Whose Parents Are Divorcing

SHAKEN FOUNDATIONS

A Resource for Young Adults Whose Parents Are Divorcing

Barbara L. Battin

Edited by Debby D. Vial

Louisville, Kentucky

© 2006 Witherspoon Press, Presbyterian Church (U.S.A.), A Corporation, Louisville, Kentucky

All rights reserved. No part of this book may be reproduced or transmitted in any form or by any means, electronic or mechanical, including photocopying, recording, or by any information storage or retrieval system, without permission from the publisher. For information or a complete listing of Witherspoon Press publications, contact Congregational Ministries Publishing, Presbyterian Church (U.S.A.), 100 Witherspoon Street, Louisville, KY 40202-1396. Additional copies of this book may be obtained by calling 1-800-524-2612.

Unless otherwise noted, Scripture quotations in this publication are from the New Revised Standard Version of the Bible, copyright © 1989 by the Division of Christian Education of the National Council of the Churches of Christ in the U.S.A. Used by permission.

Every effort has been made to trace copyrights on the materials included in this book. If any copyrighted material has nevertheless been included without permission and due acknowledgment, proper credit will be inserted in future printings after notice has been received.

Project Manager: Tricia Tedrow
Cover Art: Kristin Ellert
Cover and Interior Design: Michelle Vissing

First Edition

Published by Witherspoon Press, Congregational Ministries Publishing, in conjunction with the Presbyterian Peacemaking Program of the Congregational Ministries Division, Presbyterian Church (U.S.A.), Louisville, Kentucky

Web site address: www.pcusa.org

PRINTED IN THE UNITED STATES OF AMERICA
06 07 08 09 10 11 12 13 14 15—10 9 8 7 6 5 4 3 2 1

Library of Congress Cataloging-in-Publication Data
Battin, Barbara L.
  Shaken foundations/Barbara L. Battin ; edited by Debby D. Vial.—1st ed.
     p. cm.
  Includes bibliographical references (p. 83).
  ISBN 1-57153-022-3 (pbk. : alk. paper)
  1. Divorced people–Religious life. 2. Children of divorced parents–Religious life. 3. Divorce–Religious aspects–Christianity. I. Vial, Debby D. II Title.

BV4596.D58B38 2005
248.8'46—DC22

2005240854

DEDICATION & ACKNOWLEDGMENTS

To these children and young adults whom I love dearly, all of whom are children of divorce:

Esther, Joha, Matthew, Michael, and Patrick
Rita and Brent

With thanks to all the young adults who helped to write this resource by sharing their stories.

And more thanks to those who have shared their personal wisdom and professional knowledge:

David Battin
Gregg Dana
Ross Thompson

And still more thanks to those who have read and responded to this material and through that circle of shared wisdom have improved it immensely:

Joha Battin, Paul Beran, Amanda Craft, Bill Gilliss,
Martha Miller, Debby Vial, Jenny Vial

And with deepest appreciation for Jim Clay, who lovingly supported me in this work and who continues to help me heal my own story rising out of broken parental bonds.

—Barbara L. Battin

Initial Planning Team
Barbara L. Battin
Dennis Cobb
Amanda Craft
Bill Gilliss
Martha Miller
Mienda Uriarte
Debby Vial
Brad Wigger

Contents

Dedication & Acknowledgments v
Preface ix
Introduction x

Facing Divorce: Facts, Figures, and Feelings 1
Dealing with Divorce: Why Should You? 10
Check-in 17
Self-Care 22
Questions, Questions, Questions 31
Mad, Sad, Glad, Scared, and Other Feelings 35
Lost and Found: Grieving and Letting Go 40
Forgiveness and Reconciliation 49
Figuring Out Family Gatherings: Holidays, Graduations, Weddings, and Other Occasions . . 56
Public and Semi-public Occasions 60
Designing Your Own Relationship 64
Spiritual Growth 70
Moving On 79
Recommended Resources 83
Bibliography 84

Preface

"After wading through books and numerous studies on divorce, this is what I realized, the one true thing: Those of us who have lived through divorce can't possibly squeeze the light and shadow of our lives into a model, or a graph, or a chart. We long for stories, not theory. We crave a forum to share our experiences, not open them up for judgment. Stories—yours and mine—are what guide us, forming what author Jill Ker Conway calls our 'inner life plots,' and it is only through stories that many of us gain true insight into our own lives. We may be struggling in our intimate relationships, but when we hear of others' struggles we realize that we are not alone."[1]

—Stephanie Staal

---

1. Stephanie Staal, *The Love They Lost: Living with the Legacy of Our Parents' Divorce* (New York: Delacorte Press, 2000), pp. 5–6.

INTRODUCTION

> "Today, one out of two marriages is expected to end in divorce."[1]
> —Beth Levine

> "Demographers now tell us that a quarter of adults under the age of forty-four are children of divorce. We are talking about millions of people who are struggling with the residue of an experience that their parents would rather forget."[2]
> —Judith Wallerstein

> "We are America's first divorce generation."[3]
> —Stephanie Staal

Divorce.

This is a book about the *experience of divorce*.

This is a book about *your experience* of divorce.

This is a book about your experience of *your parents' divorce*.

Divorce statistics tell one kind of story about the experience of divorce in the United States. They tally numbers. They indicate trends. They talk in calculated terms about what is being called a *culture of divorce*. They call us to notice that the experience of divorce is affecting a significant number of people in the population, not only the primary characters in the story—the marital partners—but also the children of the marriage that ends in divorce.

There is another part of the story. It is the story of what the statistics mean for people day by day, throughout the seasons of the year and the stages of life. Stephanie Staal has taken those statistics and made a statement that indicates that the raw numbers are no longer just statistics, but have become part of a whole generation's identity. If you are reading this book, it is

---

1. Beth Levine, *Divorce: Young People Caught in the Middle* (Springfield, NJ: Enslow Publishers, Inc., 1995), p. 10.
2. Judith Wallerstein, Julia Lewis, and Sandra Blakeslee, *The Unexpected Legacy of Divorce: A 25 Year Landmark Study* (New York: Hyperion, 2000), p. xix.
3. Stephanie Staal, *The Love They Lost: Living with the Legacy of Our Parents' Divorce* (New York: Delacorte Press, 2000), p. 3.

Shaken Foundations

likely that you share that identity. As part of "America's first divorce generation," you have significant challenges to face, but you are not alone in the struggle. As Stephanie Staal's own story makes clear, these challenges are significant not only for young adults whose parents have divorced but for others in your generation and the larger society as well.

The Purpose of This Book

A lot of research has been done on children whose parents divorce during their childhood or adolescence. Good resources exist for helping young children and teens understand and cope with their parents' divorce. Less research has been done on the experience of young adults whose parents divorce during that time of their lives (ages 18–35). Very few resources exist to assist and encourage young adults in understanding their parents' divorce, in honoring and reflecting on their own experience of their parents' divorce, and in deciding how they will deal with the changes it brings to their lives. There are even fewer resources available for young adults that offer an opportunity to look at their experience from a spiritual perspective. The purpose of this resource is to give you support as you consider your part of the divorce story, as you ask questions, as you seek wisdom, as you design and live the next chapter of your life.

The Peacemaking Program of the Presbyterian Church (U.S.A.), working with offices of Young Adult Ministries and Family and Single Adult Ministries, is inviting you to use this resource to tell your story. The resource is intended to provide some general information about divorce and a lot of opportunity to reflect on your own experience. We hope your interaction with this resource will lead to a dialogue of discovery with your thoughts and feelings. We include specific tools for spiritual growth and faith development. We cannot cover all the topics that you may want to explore. However, we provide a variety of options for you for getting in touch with what you need and a list of resources for you to read further. We hope this resource will engage your heart, mind, body, and spirit. We hope it will assist you in your own healing and increase your ability to be a companion for siblings or friends as they go through the experience of divorce.

Who Will Use This Book

Primarily, we are writing this book for you—young adults who are working through the experience of their parents' divorce during their post-high school years. Throughout the book, when we speak of *you*, this is the particular person we have in mind. However, others may be listening in on this resource: your pastor or another church leader, your friends and extended family, perhaps your parents. Other listeners may include counselors, social work professionals, and mentors in educational settings. Whether you are in the primary audience or are someone listening in, we hope that, if you do find this resource helpful, you will recommend it to others.

Introduction

There is no right way to use this resource. There is no wrong way. The best way to use this resource is to do it *your way*. You choose what is helpful for you and leave the rest.

As you decide what way is best for you to use this book, be aware that setting aside time and choosing a safe personal space to read and respond is important. The material in this book is intended to help you explore your thoughts and feelings. It may raise old issues for you or bring old wounds or pains into the present. We recommend giving yourself the gift of time to address these issues without rushing. We encourage you to choose carefully either a place that will allow you to focus on these materials alone or a place where you and a trusted companion may engage in conversation about them without unnecessary interruption. If you choose to work alone, it may be helpful to identify someone with whom you can share your reflections after you have spent some time with the materials.

It's Your Story

However you read and use this book, remember: It is *your* story. It is your story behind all the statistics. And that is what matters. We hope that this resource provides an opportunity for you to reflect on your story in a way that helps you heal and gives you support to continue to "write your life story" toward a healthy, joyful, loving future.

Shaken Foundations

How to Use This Book

There are many ways to use this book. Some people will read it front to back, section by section, all the way through. Others will pick and choose the parts that most pertain to their particular needs at the moment. Still others will read and use some pieces of it now, then come back to it later to continue their reflection or to work with a different aspect of their response to their parents' divorce.

- You may want to read this book alone and do the exercises and meditations on your own.
- You may share it with a good friend, perhaps someone else who is going through or who has gone through the experience of their parents' divorce.
- You may want to talk about what you read and discover with a pastor, a teacher, a spiritual guide, a trusted family member, or a small group that reads the book together and supports one another in exploring the questions and reflections.
- You may simply read what is here and think about it from time to time or use this book as a journal in which you write about your thoughts and feelings.

Facing Divorce
Facts, Figures, and Feelings

"Getting divorced was not part of my long-term plan."
"Divorce is a process, not a single event."[1]
—Vicki Lansky

There are many reasons for divorce and many responses to it. People who marry do not plan to divorce. A majority of Americans say they value a happy marriage above all else. And yet, the facts are that in the United States there has been a 50% divorce rate for the past thirty years. 45% of marriages end within the first fifteen years. The median duration of a marriage is 7.2 years. 75% of those who divorce go on to remarry. 60% of those who remarry will divorce again.[2]

When your parents married, they did not see divorce as part of their long-term plan, but it happened. In some cases where divorce occurs, family life has been full of conflict, sometimes accompanied by violence. In these cases divorce can be a relief, a solution and resolution to immediate problems and dangers. In other cases, family life may have been stable if not a model of a healthy marriage and loving relationship. In still others, a change in one or both partners alters the dynamics of a once vibrant marriage and the relationship cannot adjust to the changes.

Every couple's divorce is unique. There are many reasons for divorce. Some reasons for divorce are:

- Incompatibility (also known as "irreconcilable differences")
- Lack or loss of intimacy (psychological and spiritual)
- Unresolved conflicts
- Erosion of mutual respect
- Infidelity
- Sexual dysfunction
- Economic instability

---

1. Vicki Lansky, *Vicki Lansky's Divorce Book for Parents: Helping Your Children Cope with Divorce and Its Aftermath* (New York: New American Library, 1989), pp. xiii and 185.
2. www.smartmarriages.com and www.divorcestatistics.org

Shaken Foundations

Facing Divorce

 Think about each of your parents and their uniqueness. Think about who each of them is and what you know about them as people.

Who were they before you knew them?

What were their lives like as children, adolescents, young adults?

Who are they now?

What are their lives like day to day?

What has hurt them?

What are their hopes and dreams?

Shaken Foundations

- Mental or physical illness
- Alcoholism and/or other drug addiction
- Domestic violence (physical abuse, sexual abuse, or emotional abuse, to spouse and/or children)
- New understanding of one's sexual orientation
- Professional priorities and considerations
- A combination of two or several of the above

While it may seem that the reasons for a divorce could be reduced to categories that you could check on a survey, there is always more to any divorce than meets the public eye. There is probably no single moment that leads to a divorce. It is a string of moments. No two stories of why a divorce happens are the same. There are variations in the most similar situations that belong only to the two individuals involved. Sometimes divorce happens because of what was said or done. Sometimes it happens because of what was not said or done. In some cases one different decision along the way could have changed the outcome. In others no one thing, or two, or even three, done differently would have made a difference. There is an invisible line in a marriage separating marital success and failure. If the line has not been crossed, it is possible to rekindle and deepen the marriage. Once the line has been crossed not much is possible to undo or redo, to make amends or create a new vision. Where that line is will be different in each marriage and for each of the partners in the marriage.

Facing Divorce

Think for a moment about the physical changes that have occurred as a result of your parents' divorce.

What effect do these changes have on your daily life?

Shaken Foundations

As each individual in God's creation is unique, so each marriage is uniquely created in the coming together of two individuals. While we can point to some commonalities, they are just that—common elements taken from the stories of real people who are each a human mystery in themselves, and who are an even more intricate mystery in their marriage. As you think about the story of your parents' marriage and your parents' divorce, it may be helpful to remember that each of them, whoever your mother or father is, is a unique part of God's creation. They both came to marriage with their own set of leftovers from their own childhood and young adulthood, with their own set of wounds, hurts, disappointments, dreams, skills, values, likes and dislikes, patterns and routines. Together they created a bond that blended the particular parts of themselves with the other person. Perhaps in marriage they also let other parts of themselves recede to the background. As you think about each of your parents and your parents together, remember that you saw only part of who they were in their marriage. You saw their marriage from the perspective of a child dealing with them primarily in their roles as parents rather than knowing them as individuals or as a couple. Only in adulthood can children come to know parents objectively.

Divorce is not a single action but a process that begins long before the papers are filed and lasts long after the decree is final. Some divorces take only a short time and are done with a great amount of mutual agreement. Some divorces are protracted, complicated by bitterness, and characterized as

---

> *Consider what mental patterns have already been challenged by your parents' divorce.*

Are there others that you know you will need to address? What else in your view of yourself or your life may need revision (re-visioning)?

Shaken Foundations

"battles." They may take years to settle. The average length of a divorce proceeding in the United States is about a year. But that is only the length of the legal proceeding. The physical, mental, emotional, and spiritual proceedings linger far beyond the time of legal disengagement. They can last a lifetime.

- The physical implications of divorce often involve moving from one house to another if not one town to another.

If one of your parents does not move, some things that were familiar in your home may leave with your other parent. You may find the physical surroundings change as the parent who retains the house makes changes. If one or both of your parents remarry, you will find new things in their homes that reflect their new partner. There may be economic implications that are part of the physical realities of the divorce . . . a move to an apartment from a house, a reduced budget for clothes, food, entertainment, and education. Divorce often has significant monetary implications that affect not only your current lifestyle, but also what is possible in the future.

- The mental implications of divorce may be more difficult to identify immediately.

Facing Divorce

We develop ways of conceptualizing life. We develop routines by which we order life. We develop images of ourselves within those concepts and routines. Those ways of thinking can become so much a part of us that until there is some challenge to them, we don't even know they exist. You may always have thought of yourself as being part of a happy family, especially compared to a friend whose parents always seemed to be fighting. When your parents divorce and your friend's parents stay married, the way you have thought about yourself and your life will be challenged. Getting used to saying "my parents are divorced" may be very difficult for you. On the other hand, if you have grown up in a family where alcoholism was a constant factor in your daily life, you may have developed coping mechanisms that look at the world as a place of uncertainty and people as untrustworthy. You may be surprised to find out that there are people who can be trusted and that you don't have to wonder when something else is going to intervene with your plans and disappoint you. You will have to adjust your thinking to fit a new reality created by the absence of a parent whose alcoholism deeply influenced your view of life.

- The emotional implications of your parents' divorce are both immediate and long-term.

Shaken Foundations

Your initial response to your parents' divorce may be anger, sadness, or gladness. It may be fear or relief, devastation or hope. You may sink into depression or experience a sense of liberation. You may feel numb at first and slowly move to being able to express your emotions. You may cry when you hear the news, and for days or weeks afterward, as you might if a loved one had died. You may think hard and analyze it as a way to protect your heart from actually feeling what is happening. You may feel as if you will drown in your tears and hide in your sadness in order not to think about the changes this will mean for you. Taking good care of yourself will be important during the adjustment to a new family lifestyle. The chapter in this book titled "Self-Care" will give you some clues to help you be aware of special needs and cues for seeking further help if that seems appropriate.

Your emotions may not always make sense or remain consistent. You may be immediately relieved without thinking about the consequences economically. Your first response may change as you move through stages of dealing with the divorce itself. It may take some years for you to come to terms with all the emotional losses from not having two parents who live together in a marriage and who create the emotional shelter of a family unit. It may take years for you to come to terms with the violence of your parents' marriage even if you were not physically hurt, or to recover from abuse if that was part of your own experience. Your parents' divorce may call into question

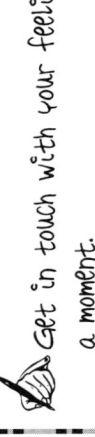 *Get in touch with your feelings for a moment.*

What do you find in your heart? What emotional tone is predominant? When you think about your parents' divorce, what is there in your emotional life that seems to be directly or indirectly related to how you are feeling and dealing with life in general?

SHAKEN FOUNDATIONS

for you the usefulness of the institution of marriage and the wisdom of making a commitment of your own. This too may take not months, but years, to work through in order for you to be able to create a healthy and happy marriage of your own.

- The spiritual implications of your parents' divorce will also take time to identify and engage.

The spiritual life is a journey that happens in relation to the elements of the physical environment, in conversation with the events of life and our mental and emotional responses to them. The spiritual journey invites us to deal not merely with the physical elements and life events, but with a dimension of life that exists both beyond and within the physical world and that threads itself through our mental functions and our emotional dealings with ourselves and others. The spiritual journey is a journey in which we develop our relationship with God, with the Sacred in life. It is where we find our identity in God and form our lives in a way that is consistent with what God intends. Some have said in short form that the spiritual journey is the journey of learning to love, not just in the romantic sense, but in the way God loves: with compassion, with justice, with mercy. Jesus showed us that this kind of loving is not dependent on our liking another person. It is always open to seeing the spark of God in everyone, even to the point of loving one's enemies.

FACING DIVORCE

 *Think about where you are in the process right now.*

What spiritual issues can you identify as part of your response to your parents' divorce? What kind of conversations have you had with God lately about their divorce and its implications on your life, on your ability to be loved and on your ability to love yourself and others?

SHAKEN FOUNDATIONS

The divorce of your parents will raise issues of a spiritual nature. You will be confronted with questions about what it really means to live as a person of God, a disciple of Jesus Christ, as you move through the stages of responding to your parents' divorce. You may struggle with what it means to love a parent who has been unfaithful to her or his marriage vows and who has hurt her or his marriage partner as a result of that. You may wrestle with how to deal with your feelings of hatred toward an abusive parent or alcoholic parent now that he or she has left and you do not need to deal daily with him or her. You may agonize about how to be fair and just and compassionate to both of your parents if they engage in tug-of-war behavior with you. You may want to shout to God about how unfair life is, or give thanks for an end to a very difficult period in your life. You may even question God's love for you or the reality of God at all if such painful things can happen. It may be the first time in your life when you are asking theological questions and wondering out loud about things about which you were certain in your childhood or youth. Nothing is out of bounds in your relationship with God, even questioning whether God is God. You may have left the church somewhere along the way. As a result of your parents' divorce, however, you are asking questions that are spiritual in nature. Dealing with the spiritual issues raised in divorce is part of the divorce process, an essential part of the divorce process.

FACING DIVORCE

Divorce happens. A lot. No two divorces are alike. Divorce is a process. Divorce has implications not only for the people who divorce, but for the whole family. This includes extended family members: grandparents, aunts, uncles, cousins, nephews, and nieces. The consequences come in as many shapes and forms as the families to whom they happen. Dealing with the implications and consequences of divorce is part of the spiritual journey. As part of the church, as part of the people of God, we make the journey together, in community. We comfort one another. We challenge one another. We are companions for one another. In this book we hope to accompany you on the journey by offering you opportunities for reflection, for considering questions, for discovering who you are because of and beyond your parents' divorce. We hope to encourage you to be creative with your life and your loving so that you may learn skills for marriage and family life that will make it possible for you to succeed where your parents failed.

Behind all the numbers are names.
Behind all the percentages are people.
Behind all the statistics are stories.
Yours is one of the stories.

Facing Divorce

Shaken Foundations

You are not alone in your experience of watching your parents divorce. As Stephanie Staal says, you are part of a "divorce generation." It may be helpful to know that there are many others wrestling with issues similar to those with which you are wrestling. On the other hand, it may also be hard to hear that divorce is so common. In writing this book we hope to help you deal with your parents' divorce so that you can write your life story in a way that leads to healthy, loving relationships in the future.

If I Could Read One Book . . .

The Love They Lost: Living with the Legacy of Our Parents' Divorce, by Stephanie Staal. While this book is written by a young adult whose parents divorced when she was in her teens, it recounts her story and addresses the issues of divorced parents in such a way that may be helpful to you.

Dealing with Divorce

Why should you?

"How young adults react to their parents' divorce is very individual, but react they will and powerfully so."[1]

—Judith Wallerstein and Sandra Blakeslee

Young adulthood, the period immediately following high school to about age thirty, is a time of important growth and development. You may still live at home. You may get an apartment on your own. You may get a job. You may go on to school either locally or in another town or state. You may be living the single life or you may marry in these years. You may have children of your own. Whatever your life looks like in terms of the outward specifics—single or married; working or in school; living in a dorm, with one of your parents, or on your own—these are significant years in your life. They present a specific set of challenges and life tasks.

Every stage of life has particular challenges and tasks to accomplish. As a baby, you had significant work to do as you began the life journey of developing into a healthy human being. In your first years, the central task was to learn to trust—to trust your caregivers and to trust life. As a toddler, the work is to learn self-confidence. Preschoolers need to learn how to balance their emerging mental and physical skills with self-control. In the elementary years, the focus is on acquiring skills and developing the confidence to use them so that they build self-esteem. Adolescents work at integrating a variety of roles into a congruent adult identity.

The challenge for you in young adulthood is to be able to establish intimate relationships. This refers to family as well as romantic relationships, friends as well as lovers. Experiencing the divorce of your parents between the ages of eighteen and thirty may have an effect on your ability to complete the work of this stage of development as you would have otherwise.

The challenge of intimacy is more than knowing all the facts, figures, and favorites about a person. It is being able and willing to share feelings with someone, and to have them share their feelings with you. It is an ongoing, ever-deepening

---

1. Judith S. Wallerstein and Sandra Blakeslee, *What About the Kids?: Raising Your Children Before, During, and After Divorce* (New York: Hyperion, 2003), p. 114.

Shaken Foundations

dialogue. Dialogue means "words across." Intimacy is talking and sharing across the great gap between your uniqueness and theirs! Intimacy asks us to lay down our shields, to open the doors of our souls, to invite others into our heart space. Intimacy requires vulnerability. Intimacy is a risk—an important, essential risk. It is necessary for the fullness of life and wholeness of personhood, for maturing as a human being.

The alternative to this is isolation. Isolation is an emotional state that can have different manifestations. You can be alone in a crowd of people whom you don't know and who don't know you. You can choose to interact with others only on a superficial level or refrain from any but the most essential interaction. If you have been hurt by those you love, if your parents have injured, betrayed, or abandoned you, you may not choose to risk intimacy. You may opt for isolation.

Intimacy is essential to healthy relationships. It is the source of joy in lasting friendships. It is a deep bond in marriage. One of the reasons marriages fail is that they lack or lose the experience of and commitment to genuine intimacy. Working through issues of broken trust that result from your parents' divorce will help you mature in this stage of life and the developmental tasks it holds.

If you have grown up in a family where learning to trust, learning to act independently, developing self-esteem, and

Dealing with Divorce

finding a clear sense of self was impeded by your family's dysfunction, your ability to deal with your parents' divorce will be more difficult. The life work of young adulthood will be more difficult as well. Even if you have moved well through these life stages and arrive at young adulthood well prepared for its next step into intimacy and committed relationships, dealing with your parents' divorce will require some additional intentional and deliberate work on your part. It will take some time, attention, and energy to sort through what happened to them and what happened to you.

Not dealing with your parents' divorce is really *not* an option. You *will* deal with it in one way or another: by avoidance or facing it; by ignoring it or learning from it; by denying the experience or integrating it into your life story in a way that allows you to continue your life in a creative manner. This book is designed to help you get in touch with the experience of your parents' divorce so that you can respond to it thoughtfully, rather than just react to it. It is intended to help you prayerfully work through the implications of your parents' divorce for your life. If you stay in the reaction stage, you remain confined by the losses of the past and the limitations of the present. Until you deal with the past and the present, they will determine the parameters of your possibilities for the future. Only as you move into the response mode do you gain the power to choose your path into a future that you design and implement.

Shaken Foundations

Dealing with Divorce

 Think about your own experiences with establishing trust and developing intimacy in relation to the following questions:

What happens if you thought while growing up that your parents had a good marriage and all of a sudden when you are twenty-three and finally out of the house, they divorce?

What happens if one of your parents whom you loved and trusted leaves and you feel abandoned?

What happens if they were unhappy all that time and stayed together "for the good of the children"?

What happens if you grew up in a household where there was little or no intimacy?

What happens if you grew up in a family where there was a high level of conflict and violence? What happens if you never saw your father being tender with your mother or your mother supporting your father?

What happens if, in the dysfunction of their relationship, you felt ignored, unappreciated, unloved?

What happens to you in young adulthood as you try to form your own relationships?

What happens to you when you think about making a commitment to someone?

What happens when you find it hard to trust, hard to know how you feel, hard to take responsibility, hard to share in a relationship?

Note: You may want to spend some time writing in a journal or talking about your reflections on these questions with a friend or counselor.

Shaken Foundations

There are many good reasons to do the inner work of dealing with your parents' divorce. Some of them are primarily personal. Completing the stages of development and growing into a healthy human being is a very good reason to deal with your parents' divorce. Addressing the effect your parents' divorce has had on your ability to form intimate relationships and find the joy of deep communion with another person is worth the time, energy, and attention it will take to do that work. The personal and interpersonal dimensions of life are important, but there is a third dimension that we need to include in the full picture of health and wholeness as a human being. It is the dimension of community.

When we talk about the ability to establish intimate relationships and to make commitments to other people (not just a life partner, but to friends and other family folk), what we are talking about is the ability to live in community with other people. We may understand this in part to be the local community, the social, political, economic systems that create and sustain the public life around us, that govern the way we use the resources of life and the earth, that are gifts of God, and that we hold in common. We must also understand this to include the world as community, as the larger context in which we live and relate and to which we are responsible.

God created the whole universe as a community. There is an original unity of which we are all a part and to which we return. In this cosmic community, all things are related. There

Dealing with Divorce

is no such thing as isolation. One definition of what we have called "sin" is to be separated from God and from the awareness of God's creation as a community. It is withholding love from one another because we feel isolated or alone, because we are afraid of risking intimacy, of risking vulnerability, of risking giving ourselves away to another, or of receiving the gift of another person into our own lives.

One of the reasons to deal with your parents' divorce is to learn to live in community. Sometimes the pain of conflicted or violent family life, of divorce and its aftermath, becomes a cycle. The wounds of childhood, adolescence, and young adulthood may cause us to shrink back from life and love, from making connections and commitments, from being active participants in the ongoing work of discovering and sustaining community in our world. Our pain may lead us to actions that become part of the problems that destroy community. Our fear may be a factor in our being passive survivors in life rather than active celebrants of life. A variety of expressions of violence toward ourselves or others (stress-related illness, shortened life span, and self-protection that breeds contempt for those who are different from us) can affect our local and global communities in such a way that they destroy the peace God intends for all human life and for the planet itself. The unexamined patterns of abusive family life or the unresolved issues of divorce can mean that they are unwittingly repeated in our lives because that is the only reality we have known.

Shaken Foundations

Dealing with Divorce

 Think about growing up in your family, about the time when your parents divorced, and about where you find yourself in the process of dealing with your parents' divorce.

Do you think you are at the beginning, in the middle, or approaching the end of your dealing with their divorce? Remember that even if you think you may be "through it," times of stress (such as life or death events, illness, emergencies, even celebrations) may send you back to deal with familiar feelings, questions, and issues from the past. With an old physical injury that has turned into a mostly forgotten scar, an unexpected movement or a change in the weather can bring soreness back to that part of the body. In a similar way, times of stress can bring back soreness to the soul. During difficult times, you may find yourself reworking something you thought was long gone and taking it to a deeper level of understanding and resolution through encountering it again.

SHAKEN FOUNDATIONS

Abused children too often become abusing parents. Children of addicted parents too often adopt addictive behaviors themselves. Children of divorce are more likely to divorce.

One of the challenges of the spiritual journey is looking at who we are in the context of our family and community life and seeking to break the cycles of violence, fear, and destruction. Even if there is deep psychological pain that results from your parents' divorce, you still have a choice about your future and the very real possibility of transformation. You have a choice in your life about whether you will use the pain you experience as an impetus to design your life differently or as an excuse for repeating the experiences of the past. The spiritual life calls us to be partners with God in transforming ourselves and our world, in the ongoing building and nurture of community, and in the ongoing creation of the universe.

Dealing with your parents' divorce may sound more personal than political, but it is a political act, a social act, an economic act, a peacemaking act. By recognizing your own patterns of violence or potential for violence, by working through your own painful experiences, by healing your own wounds, by changing your own life, by developing compassion for others who are in pain and in need of healing, you contribute to the flow of God's love in the world. You remove the barriers of pain and release the power of God's love by increasing your own ability to love yourself, your family, your friends, your neighbors, and even those whom you may consider to be enemies.

DEALING WITH DIVORCE

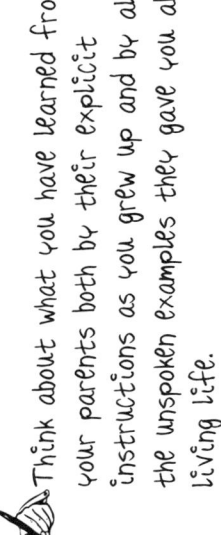

Think about what you have learned from your parents both by their explicit instructions as you grew up and by all the unspoken examples they gave you about living life.

What have you learned that you want to retain as healthy and positive for building God's community of peace in the world?

What can you identify as negative, dysfunctional, unhelpful, or destructive patterns or worldviews that you would like to eliminate?

Dealing with Divorce

📖 If I Could Read One Book . . .

The Love They Lost: Living with the Legacy of Our Parents' Divorce, by Stephanie Staal.

Shaken Foundations

Sociologists and psychologists both acknowledge that dealing with divorce in ways that examine its issues and implications has value not only for personal growth but also for social and community life. Dealing with your parents' divorce is an important, essential contribution to making peace in our world.

Check-In

"Every story of divorce is complex."[1]
—Stephanie Staal

Have you ever been asked, "How do you feel about your parents' divorce? What did you say then? What would you say today?

This chapter is designed to be a "check-in" on that question.

The questions in this section offer you a focus for reflecting on many aspects of your parents' divorce. There are no right or wrong answers. They are an opportunity to be in conversation with yourself about where you are now in relation to the event of your parents' divorce. We shared some of these questions with other young adults prior to including them in this book. One of those who responded said she found them very helpful not only in getting in touch with her feelings at the present time, but also in thinking about what she wanted to do to continue the healing process into the future.

Find a comfortable place, a quiet space alone or one in the midst of hubbub and humanity if that feels better. Give yourself the gift of some open time. Don't rush through these. You don't need to deal with all the questions at once. Remember that they are for you alone unless you choose to share them with someone else. Be aware that these questions may evoke strong feelings. You may want to read all the questions through first. You may want to take them one by one. Spaces are provided for you to write brief responses in this book. You may also choose to write your response in a journal or notebook. Perhaps you will only think them through and not write anything at all. You may want to simply read them now and respond to them later. You may want to share some or all of them with a friend, a family member, a counselor, a pastor, or even your parents.

Do what is most helpful to you.

---

1. Stephanie Staal, *The Love They Lost: Living with the Legacy of Our Parents' Divorce* (New York: Delacorte Press, 2000), p. 7.

SHAKEN FOUNDATIONS

CHECK-IN

1. What is the story of your parents' divorce? What happened? Were they separated before the divorce? Did they seek counseling before their decision to divorce? Why did they divorce?

Write a paragraph that recalls how you first heard about your parents' intent to divorce. Include what you remember about how you felt physically and emotionally when you heard the news.

OR

Try writing a poem as you think about this.

2. Have you asked either or both of your parents "What happened?" If not, why not? If so, what did they say?

3. How are you feeling right now about your parents' divorce? Consider these words as you think about this question: mad, sad, glad, afraid, anxious, ambivalent, hurt, resentful, frustrated, strong, vulnerable, confused, surprised, at peace. Circle all that apply. You may find yourself circling several words. They may even seem inconsistent or even opposite. That's okay. You may find you have a range of responses depending on the circumstances of your parents' divorce, your previous experience with their marriage, and your relationship with each parent.

Are there any other words that you would add to this list?

4. Go back and look at all the words you circled or added. What is behind each of those words?

Write a sentence or two about each of them. For example: "I'm *mad* because . . ." or "I'm *surprised* that . . ."

You may want to use crayons, markers, or paints to express your feelings.

5. How has your parents' divorce affected your relationship with your mother? your father?

6. What do you know about how the rest of your family is responding to your parents' divorce?
    Siblings
    Grandparents
    Aunts/uncles
    Other family members

7. How is your parents' divorce affecting your day-to-day life?
    Work
    School
    Friends
    Social life
    Significant relationships

SHAKEN FOUNDATIONS

CHECK-IN

8. What implications does your parents' divorce have for your own future?

   Does it affect where you feel "at home"?

   Does it affect your financial security or educational opportunity?

   Have there been changes in your relationships with your immediate family, your extended family, your friends?

   Has it changed vacation times for you?

   What impact has it had on holidays?

   How do you think it will affect life events like graduations or weddings?

9. Have either or both of your parents remarried? How do you view that relationship (healthy, happy, unhealthy, unhappy, positive, negative, etc.)? What impact has the remarriage had on you? your siblings?

10. Does your parents' divorce affect how you look at your own sense of a committed relationship?

    If you are not dating or in a relationship at this time, does your parents' divorce influence how you think about dating or falling in love or making a life commitment to someone?

    If you are currently dating or in a dating relationship with one person, does your parents' divorce have an impact on how you approach dating?

    If you are currently engaged, does your parents' divorce change how you experience your engagement?

    If you are married, does your parents' divorce raise questions for you about your own marriage?

11. Has your parents' divorce affected your understanding of God or your relationship with God?

    Has it affected how you view the church or your relationship with the church?

Shaken Foundations — Check-In

12. What has been the hardest thing for you to deal with in regard to your parents' divorce?

13. What have you "lost" as a result of your parents' divorce?

14. What are you learning about yourself as a result of your parents' divorce?

15. Have there been any "gifts" as a result of your parents' divorce?

16. Where or from whom are you receiving support as you deal with your parents' divorce?

17. Do you have any unanswered questions or wonderings about your parents' divorce? Do you need to pursue those questions with them?

18. What do you need to do . . . what do you want to do . . . to be healthy and whole as you continue on life's journey?

For Further Reflection:

When you have finished writing your responses to the questions, go back and review them.

Are there any surprises in your responses?

Were there some that were more difficult to respond to than others?

If you were going to add a question, what would it be?

Simply sit for a few minutes and think about the story these questions have evoked—your story.

Self-Care

"Be careful with your time."

"Be honest with yourself. No feeling that you have is wrong."

"Go talk to someone. Friends are great, but going to a third party that doesn't know you or your parents very well can help to shed some light on the situation that you may not have seen before."

"Find someone to talk to about it that has dealt with it before . . . Nothing is more comforting than knowing that someone understands."[1]

A first step in self-care is to assess what is happening with you right now.

- Are you reading this book because you feel as if you are "drowning in divorce," because you are in immediate need of help in dealing with your parents' decision to divorce?
- Are you in the early stages of your response to your parents' divorce? Is it a recent event?
- Are you reading this book because you have dealt with the immediate shock or the first acknowledgment of the divorce event and you want to reflect on it from some distance now that a little time has passed?
- Have you had some time to get used to this change in their lives and yours? A year or more?
- Has it been quite a while — more than a couple of years — since your parents divorced but you are still feeling the upheaval?
- If your parents divorced a while ago, did you just keep on living your life as if nothing much happened? Are you coming back to the event now, feeling that it is fresh and immediate, with all the loss seeming overwhelming or confusing or even surprising?

Whatever your situation, if you are reading this book, you will need to be "care-full" of yourself (a) as you explore your feelings, thoughts, reactions, and responses; (b) as you seek healing; and (c) as you work to write your own story for the future.

Here are some things to be concerned about as you assess your current health and well-being:

---

1. Comments from young adults responding to author's survey.

Shaken Foundations

Eating

- Are you overeating as a way to fill the empty space inside?
- Are you craving comfort food as a way to feel better for the moment because life seems too hard to handle?
- Are you not eating at all as a way of rebelling against your parents' decision?
- Are you just not interested in food because you find their decision so difficult to deal with?

Both overeating and not eating can be warning signs to which you should pay attention. Only you will know for sure what is happening, so you must be honest with yourself about what is happening with you and to you.

Sleeping

- Are you sleeping too much or too little?
- Are you sleeping more than usual as a means of escape, of not thinking about and not dealing with your parents' divorce and its consequences for your life?
- Are you having trouble getting to sleep or staying asleep all night?

Any one of these could be a symptom of depression in response to your parents' divorce. If either sleeping all the time or not sleeping well continues for a longer time than three weeks, and there are no other factors involved (like finals week or a major event in your work life), seeing your doctor would be a good idea. Some sleep disturbance is normal in response to grief about a life event such as your parents' divorce. If you become stuck in one of these patterns, consider seeking help in dealing with it.

Self-Care

Not being able to concentrate

- Is it hard to focus your mind for more than a few minutes at a time?
- Does your mind wander easily, especially to thoughts about the divorce?

Lack of ability to concentrate can also be a signal to which you should pay attention.

Change in sexual behavior

- Has your sexual activity changed as you have been focusing on your parents' divorce?
- Has your interest in sexual activity increased or diminished significantly?

Seeking comfort and/or intimacy through sexual encounter can be one way to deal with the uncertainty or emotional upset that may come when your parents divorce. It may offer immediate solace or escape, but alone it will not provide a way of working through the issues you face when your parents divorce. Avoiding sexual contact is another reaction to emotional turmoil, especially turmoil that emerges from relationships where intimacy and trust are core issues. If you suddenly find yourself not responsive to your life partner, talking about it with that person is important as is seeking help if the pattern continues for an extended period of time.

USE OF DRUGS AND ALCOHOL

- Are you experimenting with new behaviors that are not healthy? Tobacco, alcohol, drugs?
- If these are already part of your life, has your use of them increased significantly?

These changes may be indicators that you need to seek some immediate help in dealing with the changes in your life brought about by your parents' divorce or in dealing with your current life situation and future hopes.

If you recognize yourself in any of these behaviors, please consider talking with your pastor, your doctor, a school counselor, a pastoral counselor, or a therapist. God created us to be in community together and to accompany one another on our life journeys. Seeking help is not a sign of weakness, but rather a sign of strength. It is often the first step toward healing and health.

SOME SUGGESTIONS ABOUT GOOD SELF-CARE

We are whole beings: heart, mind, spirit, and body. When we respond to anything in life, we respond emotionally, intellectually, spiritually, and physically. We may have a preferred or primary way of responding according to our personality, but all the other aspects of our being respond as well. It is important both to think about your preferred mode of response and to understand and honor the other parts of your being. If you are a "head" person and usually *think* things through thoroughly as a way of responding to events, it will be important to also be aware of how you are feeling. If you tend to be *emotionally* responsive, then it may help to check in with your body to notice what is happening *physically*. If you are primarily a *physical* person in touch with your body's patterns, being aware of your *spiritual* self may be an important part of your healing process. If you are a *spiritually* focused person, remember to be aware of each of the other aspects of yourself as important sources of information about your health and well-being.

Taking time, making space, going slowly. As we said earlier, divorce is a process. Your parents' divorce did not happen overnight, even though it may have been a shock to one of your parents or a surprise to you. Your response to this change and the healing that will allow you to embrace the future and design your own life story will not happen overnight either.

Give yourself time. Don't try to rush through the stages of grief (spend some time with the chapter titled "Lost and Found: Grieving and Letting Go," if you have not read it yet). Genuine "letting go" is not a single act, but a gradual process.

Give yourself space. In this time of dealing with your parents' divorce, it is important to make psychological space in your ordinary routines to work through the issues the divorce raises for you. A thousand things are available to each of us in any one moment of life. There are the necessary things of life like school or work, and the variety of entertainment options: television, movies, sports. There is e-mail and the Web. Time with friends and time with family or significant others can also fill your days. Life can get very crowded. Your calendar can fill up so that there is no white space left. Sometimes just doing nothing and not focusing on anything can take up a lot of space in life. Dealing with your parents' divorce will require some space in your life. It will require a commitment of attentiveness to what has happened in your life and to yourself as you respond to what has happened.

Go slowly. Be kind to yourself. Be gentle with yourself. If you are just at the beginning of dealing with your parents' divorce (especially if this has been a surprise to you), you may want to limit how much you say "yes" to others in the immediate future. Doing too much may be a way of avoiding the current reality. Remember that you are in charge of your life and the author of your own story. Taking good care of yourself now may be one way of writing a healthy story in the future.

Stay active. This may sound like the exact opposite of what we have just said. It is not. For some people, the temptation will be to withdraw from life, to pull back, to cancel everything on the calendar, to retreat from outside events. As with most things in life, what is needed is not an either/or approach, but a both/and approach. There is a need for personal time and space, but this doesn't mean complete abdication of responsibility, or hibernation, or refusal to participate in life. Beware of going too far in either direction—overcommitment or isolation. There are three specific parts of staying active:

Exercise. Our emotional responses (recognized or unrecognized) have a chemical component that is released into our bodies. Some of these are positive chemicals like endorphins, as when we experience joy, hope, and love. Other chemicals have more negative effects on our bodies—adrenaline, for instance. It is good for a quick getaway in an emergency situation, but if it sits in the body for a long time, it is not healthy for the body. One of the ways to flush out negative chemicals and release positive chemicals in our bodies is to exercise.

Get up. Get out. Walk. Run. Hike. Swim. Garden. Go to the gym. Play tennis, soccer, handball, basketball.

Shaken Foundations

Have fun. Yes. Have fun. Have a good time. Do something you deeply enjoy. You may not really feel like going out with friends or engaging in a favorite activity. Do it anyway. Getting out and about can remind you that there is more to life—and more to *your* life—than this one event. It can also give you a needed break from thinking about some of the things you need to think about.

Laugh. Whenever you can, whenever it can be genuine—*laugh*, the more the better. It is good for the soul and good for your body. Laughter has been called "the best medicine." Many doctors would agree. Laughter massages the torso and stimulates blood flow that helps to clean out your body chemistry like exercise does. Rent a comedy movie, read a funny book, or listen to the jokes your best friend tells—and let yourself laugh.

You are what you eat. Remember that good nutrition not only helps the body, but also the mind, the heart, and the spirit. Too much caffeine can make you hyper, irritable, and interrupt that important sleep. Sugar can give you a quick high, but plummet you to just as sudden a low.

Alcohol is a depressant. If you are already feeling a bit down, it will send you down further.

Guides for healthy eating apply especially when a crisis comes in life. Regular and balanced meals are always important. If you eat alone, try lighting a candle on the table and eating slowly. If you eat with friends or family, give thanks for their

Self-Care

companionship. *Companion* comes from the French and means "with bread." Sharing the bread of life with friends and family may not add vitamins to your meal, but it can add vitality to it!

Monitor your "self-talk." We all talk to ourselves all the time, though it may not be out loud. We all have voices inside our heads that are giving us messages about who we are, what we should do or not do, whether we are doing well or poorly, whether we are loved or not. The messages are sometimes left over from childhood, echoes of the voices of a parent or teacher or of a group of kids with whom we hung out, or even of our own internalized cultural norms or expectations. They can be positive or negative. Sometimes we are aware of them as part of our life script and sometimes not. Sometimes they are even contradictory. Yes. No. Yes. Sometimes it feels as if there is a committee meeting in our heads!

The conversations in our heads, with ourselves, are almost endless. If we listen in on our own conversations, we can learn a lot about where we really are and what we really think about our lives.

Emptying the Trash

If we have a lot of negative messages about ourselves, they may pop up like ads on our computer screens when we find ourselves in a vulnerable place in life. We may even have done a lot of psychological or spiritual work to deal with the negative messages we received growing up, but they can resurface from somewhere deep within and return from the deleted category to an active file through which we process information about what is currently happening. This inner voice, this kind of internal conversation, is often called trash talk. Trash talk is not part of responsible self-evaluation that acknowledges that we all fall short at times, that we are incomplete human beings, and that we are all in process. Trash talk simply applies a negative perspective to whatever is happening and personalizes it. It says: "It's all my fault." "I'm a failure." "I'm not good at anything." "I am not perfect." "I am not lovable."

If you find yourself with a lot of trash talk in this time of dealing with your parents' divorce, you may want to enlist the help of a trusted friend or professional counselor to look at this pattern. Having become aware of it, you may also be able to work to stop the behavior on your own and replace it with a healthy self-image that empowers you to accept yourself as you are and to grow into the person you want to be.

Affirmations. Sometimes we all need reminders that we are loved, capable, valuable. One way to move from trash talk to a healthy empowerment of self is to use a set of affirmations. You could think about these as Post-it® notes for the soul. These may be short sayings or pieces of wisdom, a verse from the Bible, or some other source that makes a positive statement about life. Sometimes it is helpful to write this on a real paper Post-it® note and stick on the bathroom mirror to remind yourself each morning of what you intend to do or be during the day. This may be some truth about yourself that you want to remember. At the end of the day, it will be there to help you think about how you lived out that intention for that day. You could also memorize a short sentence or phrase and use it like a mantra that you repeat over and over to yourself throughout the day.

Take a moment now to think of one affirmation you could use to remind yourself that you are an unrepeatable mystery with creative potential, loved by God who created you and who placed you in the community of the universe.

Creativity. Part of caring for yourself in the wake of divorce, in the aftermath of the death of a marriage relationship to which you had an intimate connection, can be taking the time to engage in creativity that deepens your relationship with yourself and with God. Divorce, whether it is necessary and eventually positive, deeply destructive, or somewhere in between, marks the breaking of a marriage and of marriage vows. At some point, something that at one time held life and love became unworkable or empty, and died. One of the affirmations of the Christian faith is that life can come from death. This is part of God's design for creation. The seasons flow from the dead of winter into the new life of spring. The cycle of summer lushness and autumn harvest flow into fallowness that once again becomes fruitful. This is the resurrection message at the core of the Easter story.

Take a moment right now and check-in with yourself.

Are you aware of any trash talk in your conversations with yourself?

What are your inner voices saying about yourself?

You may want to make a list in the margins of the things you say to yourself that qualify as trash talk. You may want to write in a journal about where these messages come from and record the times and contexts when they pop up most frequently. Being aware of trash talk is the first step in deleting it. Deciding to empty the trash is the second step.

SHAKEN FOUNDATIONS

Resurrection is real for our lives. The apostle Paul says that "all things work together for good for those who love God" (Romans 8:28).

Journal writing, painting, writing poetry, quilting, woodcarving, sculpting, gardening, making music, dancing, cooking, and other creative endeavors have the power to affirm life. In the midst of chaos, they help to bring order to our minds, hearts, spirits, and even our bodies. They provide opportunities for reflection on what has been. Through a gentle contemplative meditation that happens as we work with our hands or bodies, our inner thoughts can rise to awareness while we work. Creative activities provide a space for us to hope and dream and envision the future. They can help us know ourselves better. They can open a spiritual window to God. They can help us heal. (The chapter titled "Spiritual Growth" has further suggestions for this.)

Talk to someone. When the world falls apart, or when it changes significantly (even for the better), talking to someone about what has happened is important. Nelle Morton tells us that when people listen to us in a way that engages their whole beings with our story, they "hear us" into speech.[2] They help us tell the story of what happened to us — the facts, but more than the facts. They help us to hear our own story beyond the facts to the feelings, to the depths, to the pain of past and present. They help us to claim our story as our own, to learn its lessons,

SELF-CARE

to seek its gifts, to acknowledge our wounds, to allow our healing.

Find someone with whom you can take the time to share your story in its fullness, who will help you hold your spoken words and the silent pauses that punctuate them as if they were precious objects in need of gentle care. Seek out a close friend, a trusted family member, a mentor, a pastor, a counselor, a spiritual guide.

Come to terms with the issue of control. Your parents' divorce was out of your control. You had no control and yet you live with the consequences. The feeling of being out of control can be frightening, especially in a culture that puts a lot of emphasis on being in control. Fear can lead us to want to control everything. Because we live in a vibrant, ever-changing universe and exist in an intricately woven community of both human beings and all created things, maintaining full control of our lives is not possible. No matter how well we plan or how much we anticipate, compensate, and correct the trajectory of our dreams, we cannot control all of what life brings our way. However, we do have a choice about how we respond to what life brings. Stephanie Staal says: " . . . while we cannot choose our past, we can choose our future."[3] There is truth in the saying: *"Change is. Growth is optional."*

It may be helpful to think for a moment about the places in which you can influence the outcomes of life and then those

---

2. Nelle Morton, *The Journey Is Home* (Boston: Beacon Press, 1985), pp. 127–129.
3. Stephanie Staal, *The Love They Lost: Living with the Legacy of Our Parents' Divorce* (New York: Delacorte Press, 2000), p. 11.

places where you can't. In your mind, create a great bubble and put in it those places that you have some choice or influence. Now, look at the list of places where you don't have that option. See if you can relax, and let them be. Concentrate on what is possible, rather than on what is not possible.

Be good to yourself. Once in a while, treat yourself to something you might not ordinarily do. Get a massage. Eat at a favorite restaurant. Check out a book you have wanted to read and give yourself the time to enjoy it. Bring home a new CD and listen to it right away. Take the afternoon off and go for a leisurely walk. Be gentle with yourself—so that you can be gentle with others.

 For Your Reflection:

What do I need to do to care for myself in a responsible and mature way during this time of upheaval in my life?

What is most important for me to do immediately to care for my body and my soul?

What are the things I need to do daily, weekly, and monthly to seek healing and to be healthy?

QUESTIONS, QUESTIONS, QUESTIONS

"... have patience with everything that remains unsolved in your heart.
Try to love the questions themselves..."[1]

—Ranier Maria Rilke

One of the most natural and common responses to the divorce of one's parents is questions.

WHY?
Why me?
Why now?
Why not sooner?
Why after all these years?
Is it my fault?
Whose fault is it?
What really happened?
Do I have to take sides?
How do I stay out of the middle?
Did they ever really love each other?
Do they still love me?
Is it possible they may get back together?
How do I relate to my parents now?
How will my parents relate to me now?
What do I tell my friends?
What will happen to me?
How can I trust someone I love?
Does this mean I will get divorced too?
What can I do so that this doesn't happen to me?
What does God think of this?
Why didn't God stop this?
Why didn't God make this easier?
What does the Bible say about divorce?
What does the church think of this?
Is the church a safe place to talk about this?

---

1. Ranier Maria Rilke, *Letters to a Young Poet*, tr. Joan M. Burnham (Novato, CA: New World Library, 2000), p. 35.

SHAKEN FOUNDATIONS

Take a moment to read these questions again. Which ones have you asked? Are there questions you have asked that are not included in the list? Add those to the list.

When you have a complete list, you may want to put a check next to the ones with which you identify the most. You may want to make some notes in the margins or use a set of symbols for the ones that are particularly yours (an ! or an * or a + or lots of ????? for emphasis). You may want to mark the list by putting a symbol by questions that you seem to have resolved through conversation with your parents, by obtaining information from family members, or in working through this part of your life story with a pastor, counselor, mentor, or friend. You may want to put another symbol by those that remain unresolved.

Give yourself a little time and space to just sit with this list and your markings. What questions seem to come back again and again? What question keeps tugging at your mind as if it won't let go? Is there any pattern to the questions that are most persistent for you? Do your questions, either what you are asking or the way you are asking them, give you some clue as to the issues on which you may need to focus so that healing may take place and you can move on in your life?

Like so many things on the journey of life, questions can be either a curse or a blessing, either a way of shutting down or of opening up, either a kind of prison holding us back from life or an opportunity for freedom to move on with life. Questions can drive us crazy. Questions can help us heal. Like so many things on the journey of life, how we approach them makes the difference.

QUESTIONS, QUESTIONS, QUESTIONS

Questions can drive us crazy. If we approach the questions that rise naturally out of responding to the experience of divorce — or any other event in life about which we had little or no say and certainly no control — as a way to gain some control, then they may drive us crazy. If we keep asking more and more questions, pursuing information and trying to pin down answers so that we can figure it all out, we are very likely to fail miserably and feel worse about whatever has happened. Figuring it all out is one more way of describing our need to control not only our own lives, but other people's lives as well. We think that if we can just figure it all out, we can fix it. Perhaps we can mend what is broken. We can turn back the clock to before the event, like some time machine that we have seen in a movie, and perhaps change the outcome. If we can just understand what went wrong, perhaps we can make it right.

One of the basic truths of life is that none of us can be in control. We are not in control of other people's lives. We are not in control of our own. We cannot control what other people do. We cannot control what happens to us. We can only choose how we will respond.

God created the whole world as a community. We are all in this together. We are in a flow of actions and reactions and responses to specific events and to life itself. We are in a great

32

Shaken Foundations

dance of life in which what each of us does matters *because* we are all related to one another, *because* we are not isolated individuals responsible only for ourselves, because our lives are woven together like strands of yarn in a great tapestry that are an ongoing creation of God. How this happens is ultimately a mystery.

If we approach our list of questions as a way of solving or getting rid of the mystery, not only will we not succeed, but we will live in an illusion. We will live in an unreality that will not lead to healing and wholeness and new life, but will confine us to the past like a prison, not because the past will not let us go, but because we will not let go of the past.

Questions can help us heal. The poet Rilke encourages us to love the questions of life, to remain open to those things in life that we cannot solve. Life is not a problem to be solved, but a mystery to be lived. When we ask questions of life, of its particular events and personal challenges, not to control the mystery or to eradicate the mystery but to wonder at it, to embrace it, to dwell in it and seek its wisdom, then our questions have the potential to help us heal. Questions then become a means of being open to learning and growing, to transformation and wisdom. Then questions enable us to meet the experiences of our lives in a way that acknowledges both our vulnerability and our power. When we are willing to take in the experience through our questions, to meet it, to dialogue with it, our encounter with it becomes a sacred quest that leads

Questions, Questions, Questions

us to new life rather than a conquest that can shut us down, harden our hearts, and block our willingness to learn and live differently.

Approaching questions in this way does not mean that we don't seek information or resolution to the questions. It means that the way we go at the asking holds the questions a bit more lightly, a bit more loosely, even a bit more lovingly. When we ask questions in this way, we are willing to "ponder them in our hearts" in a way that seeks not only "the facts and just the facts," but a holistic picture that gives us the larger context for the facts. When we ask questions in a way that creates space for more than one perspective, for more than one opinion, even for more than one thing to be truthful, we enlarge our hearts to include multiple and complex causes, and more than one possibility for the future. And that is called *freedom*. The past is not a prison that seems to bind us. It becomes a platform from which we may look at the great landscape of life and choose our own direction in the future. The power to choose life, to choose how we will live our lives from wherever we are in the present moment, is a mark of what may be called resurrection living, a mark of healthy spiritual living as shown to us in the life of Jesus Christ.

In all of the questioning you do as you reflect on your parents' divorce, there will be two kinds of questions. There will be questions to which you may find answers and receive responses. There also will be questions to which there are no

Shaken Foundations

answers or responses, no matter how hard you look, no matter how much you think them through, no matter how diligent you are in pursuing them. However, if you approach your questions with an intent to seek wisdom beyond information, the gift of God's grace beyond getting it right, and growth in your own life and faith beyond fixing what has broken, the questions can lead you to a deeper sense of yourself and a more mature way of living your life.

Questions, Questions, Questions

 *For Your Reflection:*

Go back now and look again at your own list of questions. Think about how you are asking those questions.

Are you looking for answers that will allow you to feel in control?

Are you seeking responses that will bring you wisdom, deepen your compassion, enlarge your heart, and empower you to live intentionally and creatively in the future?

Mad, Sad, Glad, Scared, and Other Feelings

"What you have to understand about me is that I'm able to cut off feelings instantly when they hurt. My feelings are there but it's hard for me to reach them. As a child I hardly knew what it was like to cry. Basically I still feel out of touch with my feelings. If you were to tell me right now that my lover died, I would not have feeling until tomorrow."¹

—"Lisa," quoted by Judith Wallerstein, Julia Lewis, and Sandra Blakeslee

For some people, feeling—good, bad, up, down, mad, sad, glad, scared—is very natural and easy. For others, feeling may be a strange land. Their heads protect their hearts. They think things through but keep a distance from their feelings. Some people are simply numb in the face of deep emotional trauma and pain.

God created us as whole beings. God gave us the ability to feel and to think. Both are appropriate and essential responses to the experience of divorce. Both are required parts of the healing process. Much of this book invites you to *think* about where you are and what you are doing and where you want to go in the future. This section invites you to *feel*, to get and be in touch with your feelings for a while and to learn to listen to your heart, to seek its wisdom for your life, and especially for your healing in the present as you deal with your parents' divorce and its effect on your life.

As you move through the experience of your parents' divorce,

it may be very helpful for you to be aware of whether you are generally responding with your heart or your head. Being in touch with your feelings as you respond, acknowledging them, experiencing them, and honoring them as part of your story of their divorce is important. It can help you deal appropriately with your feelings in the present and help you recognize them in the future when they return, either as a memory or as a fresh response in another situation.

The experience of your parents' divorce can evoke all sorts of feelings. You may be mad one moment, sad the next, and even glad sometimes. You may be afraid or confused or have a wave of peace flow over you without any clear reason for it. Stopping the flow of emotions is not healthy or helpful. Recognizing emotions, understanding what evokes them, and deciding how to express them responsibly is part of the healing process, and can bring a gift of wisdom as you move ahead in life.

1. Judith Wallerstein, Julia Lewis, and Sandra Blakeslee, *The Unexpected Legacy of Divorce: A 25 Year Landmark Study* (New York: Hyperion, 2000). p. 279.

Shaken Foundations

Mad, Sad, Glad, Scared, and Other Feelings

> Take a few moments and ask yourself, "How do I respond most often to the events of life?"

Feeling .... **Thinking**

Where would you place yourself between these two ways of responding?

How long does it take you to know how you feel about something?

How long does it take you to know what you think about something?

How easily do you express your feelings? Very easily? Not very easily? Not at all?

With whom do you share your feelings?

Is it easier for you to express happy/glad feelings, or sad feelings?

How do you deal with grieving and loss?

What happens when you are mad or angry about something?

How long does it take you to get in touch with being angry?

Shaken Foundations

Mad, Sad, Glad, Scared, and Other Feelings

What do you do with your anger when you feel angry?

Do you stuff it away? Do you express it?

How do you express your anger?

Directly, by going to the person with whom you are angry?

Indirectly, by telling other people, but not that person, about your anger?

Passive-aggressively, by saying or doing something to the person with whom you are angry that is not directly expressive of or related to the incident that made you angry?

By acting on things instead of people (beating pillows or throwing things)?

What happens when you are afraid? What do you do with your fear?

Can you think of an experience where you were joyful?

What makes you laugh?

When do you feel "at peace"? Is this tied to a place or a person or an experience?

Shaken Foundations

Mad, Sad, Glad, Scared, and Other Feelings

Mad, sad, glad, afraid, anxious, ambivalent, hurt, resentful, relieved, frustrated, confused, strong, vulnerable, surprised, at peace.

Not all of these are technically "emotions," but they are natural and common responses to events like divorce. Take a moment now to look at the list above. Circle the feelings that have been part of your response to your parents' divorce. Look at each one you circled. See if you can remember when you first felt that feeling in regard to your parents' divorce . . . and how often you have felt it. You may want to make some notes in the margins or in a journal you keep to jot down a few reflections as they arise.

When you have spent a little time with each of the feelings you circled and have a sense of them in the context of your experience of your parents' divorce, see if you can develop a dialogue with each of your feelings. See if you can start a conversation with each feeling and go a little deeper into knowing yourself and your responses by getting to know your feelings better.

For instance:

Mad. You could ask first what specifically is it that makes you so angry about your parents' divorce. Are you more angry with one of your parents than the other? Are you more angry than sad? Is your anger related to fear in any way?

Sad. Sadness is a primary response to grieving and loss. As you sit with your sadness, you may feel like asking it a bunch of questions. You may just want to notice how it feels and perhaps work with "My sadness feels like . . ." You may want to consider what you have lost or what you have learned that has brought on the sadness.

Glad. If you find yourself glad or at least relieved about your parents' divorce, you may want to start your conversation with yourself by asking simply, "why?" and listing the reasons. You may also want to check in with yourself to see if any part of you feels bad about feeling glad. In some cases, feeling relieved or glad may be an appropriate response. In others, if you find yourself glad because the divorce hurts someone who hurt you, perhaps you will want to spend some more time getting in touch with your anger and asking about the relationship between your glad and mad feelings.

Afraid. When you feel fearful, it is a good practice to engage in a dialogue with your fear that asks as many questions as possible about that fear. You may start out by asking, "What am I afraid of?" and hear yourself say something like, "I am afraid that Mom and Dad won't be there when I need them." See if you can go underneath what you find as your first sense of fear and ask again, "What am I afraid of?" You may hear yourself say something like, "I am afraid that they won't love me anymore." That may seem like all there is, but ask yourself again, "What am I afraid of?" You may hear yourself say something like, "I am afraid I am unlovable." Or underneath that, "I am afraid that I may not be capable of loving." Or "I

Shaken Foundations

am afraid that what happened to their love for one another will happen to me if I love someone." Keep asking the question until no more responses that feel *right* or *real* rise in response to your questioning.

It may not seem so at first, but your emotions are a gift of your humanity. The ability to feel deeply about life is a gift. Paying attention to our emotions can bring healing and wisdom. The psalm writers knew this. The word *psalm* comes from the word *song*. Like our own country western songs, the psalms speak clearly about the ups and downs of life. You may want to read some of the psalms as you go through this time. They are full of laments about things that happen in life and they are full of praise for the gift and gifts of life. Sometimes woefulness and praise occur in the same psalm!

Some of the psalms present life more as a mystery that evokes our awe rather than as a puzzle that we can solve. The psalms also point us to the Great Mystery, to God who hears our cries and our rejoicings, who cares for our lives and what happens to us, whose hope for us is always healing, whose intent for us is always wholeness. The psalms are prayerful approaches to God, the Sacred One of life, which seek God in times of both trouble and celebration. They model for us a relationship with God that encourages us to walk with God as our companion in all circumstances of life.

Mad, Sad, Glad, Scared, and Other Feelings

If I Could Read One Book....

Psalms of Lament, by Ann Weems. Ann Weems, a Presbyterian elder, wrote this book of psalms after the death of her twenty-one-year-old son, Todd. They offer a model for expressing our deepest feelings in prayer to our God, who is large enough to receive all our pain, hurt, anger, and sorrow.

For Your Reflection:

Read a few psalms where the writers express themselves freely and reflect a full range of emotional response to life's events and experiences. Psalms 22, 27, and 40 are psalms like this. You may read them in the New Revised Standard Version or you may want to try *Psalms for Praying: An Invitation to Wholeness* by Nan C. Merrill.

Try writing your own psalm of praise, wailing, gratitude, anger, confusion, gladness, fearfulness, or restoration.

Lost and Found

GRIEVING AND LETTING GO

"Resolving grief means letting go."[1]
—Judith Wallerstein and Sandra Blakeslee

Divorce is a kind of death. Divorce is the death of a marriage, the loss of a vision of a life together. It is a deep loss, not only to the two people directly involved, but also to those who have been a part of the marriage: children, extended family, and friends. When divorce happens, grief is an appropriate response. Even if you feel that your parents' divorce is necessary, that it is a good thing for each of them and for you and your family, you may find yourself experiencing grief, the loss of traditional family either in reality or in what you dreamed it might one day be.

Grieving is not one prescribed experience. It takes as many forms as there are people who experience grief in response to the physical death of a loved one, a divorce, the loss of a dream or sense of self, or of an opportunity in life. There are no rules for grieving, no assurance that if you follow a particular pattern you will come through it more or less easily. There is no standard time that it "should" take. There are some common characteristics to the grieving process gathered from many people's experiences.

Denial. Bargaining. Anger. Sadness. Acceptance. Elisabeth Kübler-Ross identified these as stages of grief. This may give the impression that they will happen in order or that they must be accomplished in order. It may suggest that it is possible to complete one stage and move on to the next, never returning to the previous one. More likely, what Kübler-Ross called stages are like rooms in a house that we visit in the grieving process. When we enter the house of grief, we may go first into one room and be there awhile, then move to another, then return to the first before entering a third. This journey through grief can be quite confusing. It may take several visits

1. Judith Wallerstein and Sandra Blakeslee, *What About the Kids?: Raising Your Children Before, During, and After Divorce* (New York: Hyperion, 2003), p. 8.

to a particular room before one ever moves into the fourth or fifth. It is possible to reach the room of acceptance one day and feel finished with the grieving process, then be surprised to wake one day a month, a year, or several years later with a deep sense of sadness or feeling a wave of anger you thought you had left behind long ago.

Divorce, as we have said, is a process. It does not happen in a moment or overnight, even if the specific news of it is a surprise. Grieving the divorce of one's parents is also a process. It will not be completed overnight or in a few weeks, or even a few months. The first year of living with the changes that come from divorce will hold many specific opportunities to assess what has been lost. Birthdays, holidays, vacations, anniversaries, and special occasions all may evoke feelings related to the grieving process, sometimes in a mix of emotions that may seem contradictory and overwhelming. In addition, the most ordinary day may hold a variety of emotions. A week or a month may be colored by a particular part of the grieving process. Sometimes when you least expect it, you will feel angry or sad or engage in the wishful thinking of bargaining or denial. It may be triggered by something that seems totally unrelated to your parents, to their marriage, or to their divorce, but it strikes you in your heart in a way that connects to your deep sadness, buried anger, or confusion over why this happened to you.

If your parents separated before their divorce, you may have a shorter or different experience of the grieving process when the legal action is finally taken. You may already have experienced many of the grieving responses that were just identified. The final action may seem anti-climactic. However, even with a time of separation prior to the legal dissolution of your parents' marriage, there may be a need for closure, for grieving what you have lost. That may be especially important if you have hoped all along that the day of final dissolution would never come.

What helps? Knowing the five characteristics of grieving is a start. Getting in touch with how they feel in your life is a good next step. Learning to notice what you are feeling at a particular time is important. Noticing what seems to consistently evoke a particular feeling or response is also important. Deciding what you will do with your grieving is a creative way of dealing with your parents' divorce. It can alleviate a sense of helplessness or powerlessness and assist you in your healing so that you can go ahead into your own future.

Shaken Foundations

Look again at the five characteristics of grief.

Denial. Denial says, "No! This can't be happening—to them, to me." This can be a way of pushing away the experience, an expression of not wanting it to be real. Denial is often the first response to the news about divorce, but it also can happen later in the grieving process.

Have you experienced denial as part of grieving your parents' divorce?

What did it feel like? How did it express itself?

Lost and Found

Bargaining. Bargaining involves the fantasy thinking we talked about in the chapter titled "Dealing with Divorce." It seeks to put things back in order, to return them to their previous arrangements. Bargaining may never be spoken out loud to your parents. It may only exist in the ongoing conversation in your head. It says things like, "If I quit college and come home, they will get back together." "If I move out of the house, they will have more time for each other and they won't divorce." "If I just get my life together, they will love each other again." "If they will just stay together until I graduate (or am married or my baby is born), they will discover they want to stay married." "Please, God, if my parents will just stay together, I will do what you want me to do."

Do you recognize bargaining as part of your own grieving process?

If so, what have you said to yourself or God or your parents that you think constitutes bargaining?

Anger. You know what anger feels like. It can be a "slow burn" or a violent outburst. It can creep up on you and rise slowly to the surface or it can strike like lightning. For some people, anger is a deep river that flows in them underneath the surface of everything they do. For others anger is like a thunderstorm that rages for a short time and then passes. Some people express their anger easily. Others have a very difficult time expressing it. Some people hold their anger in and use passive–aggressive behavior that becomes an indirect punishment for another person without ever having spoken their feelings. Others let anger brew to the point of violence—violence in words, physical violence, or even violence turned against themselves. Another way of dealing with anger is to acknowledge feelings in a way that can resolve conflict, mend a relationship, or heal a situation.

Some people think anger is a bad thing and won't even admit they are angry.

Anger is neither bad nor good. Anger is. It is okay to be angry. Anger rises when we feel hurt or threatened or afraid. We seldom have a choice about being angry. We always have a choice about how we express anger. Dealing creatively and respectfully with our anger is important. Anger can become a helpful agent, an important ally, in the grieving process. It helps us assess where we hurt, whether we feel threatened, or what we fear as a consequence of someone else's actions or our own, and that includes the divorce of parents.

 Anger:

Can you identify a time when you felt very very angry with your parents about their decision to divorce?

How would you describe your style of anger? (slow burn or outburst, river or thunderstorm, etc.)

How do you think others would describe the way you express your anger?

How much anger do you have? A little? A lot? To whom or where is it directed?

Is there something that can stimulate or evoke your anger?

How do you channel your anger? Do you express it directly? snidely? aggressively? violently? creatively? respectfully?

In general, how do you feel about your anger? Is there anything you want to change about how you deal with it or express it?

Shaken Foundations

Sadness. Everyone feels sad from time to time. In responding to your parents' divorce, you may find yourself feeling overwhelmed with sadness. It may feel like a cloud around you or as if you are being submerged in water. It may be like a chilly breeze that blows from time to time or a feeling of hollowness, a deep hole inside, or an empty space. Sadness is a natural response to loss. Usually, it doesn't help to try to shoo it away. But it is not healthy to stew in sadness for an extended period of time, to wallow in it, to wrap it like a cloak around you so that it colors everything else you experience. It is important to find a balance between trying to stay cheerful through it all, which may be a mark of denial, and sinking to the depths, which may be a mark of depression.

Your friends, family, maybe even your parents may try to cheer you up. Sometimes that is helpful and sometimes it is not. It is okay to let them know when it is and when it is not helpful. Sometimes anger is a cover for sadness. Then it is important to get beneath the anger to acknowledge and deal with the sadness that isn't being felt fully. Sometimes tears may flow as part of our expression of sadness (or anger). At other times, we will need to name the sadness by talking to a friend and getting the feelings out in the open where we can see them and share them. At still other times, we just need to sit awhile in the room of sadness as a way of honoring our experience. Staying there forever, though, will not lead to healing. If your sadness goes on and on, it may be a sign that

Lost and Found

you need to talk to your pastor, a counselor, or your doctor. You may need some help in working through the sadness (and other parts of the grieving process). Talking with a counselor or pastor may assist you in doing that. In some cases, medication may be needed if your sadness becomes the medical condition of depression. Asking for help is a healthy response to dealing with your parents' divorce.

 Sadness:

What is your experience of sadness in regard to your parents' divorce?

What makes you saddest about their decision to divorce?

What events or situations evoke the sadness?

What do you do with the sadness when it comes? Talk with someone? Bury it? Write about it in a journal? Cry?

Shaken Foundations

Acceptance. There are moments in the grieving process when you will feel that the divorce has happened, what once was real is now gone, and it is time to get on with life. This doesn't mean that all the feelings about the divorce have been worked through or that everything—or anything—is fixed. This doesn't mean that life has become settled again or that all the lessons of the event have been learned. The divorce took time to happen. It will continue to have a ripple effect and raise questions and emotions far into the future. But there are moments when it may begin to feel less oppressive, overwhelming, or all consuming. You may even just get tired of it as a central part of your life. It may become like a new piece of furniture moved into your living room. At first, you are very aware of it and have to walk around it carefully in order not to bump your knee or stub your toe. Gradually, you get used to it and it becomes part of the room. It doesn't disappear, but it becomes integrated into the total makeup of life.

The feeling of acceptance may include a sense of peace about the divorce and/or your future beyond it. It may mean seeing the necessity of the divorce even if you still don't like that necessity. It may be finding something in it that is a gift or a grace from God, something that frees you or strengthens you or stirs you to creativity. It may be simply saying, "This is what is. I cannot change it. I will move on from here with a clear head and a compassionate heart."

Acceptance may come first in flashes, small moments of release of tension and relaxing into the new reality of life. It may visit for a time and then suddenly disappear. Sometimes the pattern of acceptance is that it is a steady growth. Sometimes it may seem like climbing a mountain where there are lots of switchbacks. It seems as if you keep seeing the same thing over and over again. Then suddenly you find yourself at the top and are able to look out over the whole experience and come to terms with it. Sometimes acceptance may come for a short period, disappear, return for a longer time, disappear again, and repeat this pattern until one day you realize you live more in the acceptance zone than in denial, anger, bargaining, or sadness.

Remember, there is no set time in which you must accomplish acceptance. It takes each person a different amount of time to come to the place where acceptance feels like the norm and other parts of the grieving process are blips on the screen rather than the whole picture.

SHAKEN FOUNDATIONS

LOST AND FOUND

You may come to the end of this section and think, "Been there. Done that." If so, good for you. You may be at the place where you have had time to grieve. You may have come through the initial response to your parents' divorce. You may have done the hard work of confronting the reality that the past is gone and something new must emerge. If so, you may be ready to let go.

You may understand the divorce as a necessary step for greater overall health and happiness of the people involved. If so, the grieving may be a little less intense, and a little shorter in duration. You may be eager to get on with life. If so, you may be ready to let go.

Sometimes most of the grieving happens before the divorce. Even before the divorce is announced or is final, your parents and you and your siblings may have gone through the stages or rooms of denial, bargaining, anger, sadness, and acceptance. The divorce itself may be anticlimactic. However, that doesn't mean you are finished with it. There is still a need to let go, to reorient your life, and to revision the future.

Letting go is not the same as grieving. Grieving still focuses on the experience of the divorce. Letting go acknowledges the need to spend time honoring what has happened to your parents and to you. It includes taking time to think about the past and what led up to the divorce. It asks for careful conversation with yourself and perhaps a friend or professional counselor in which you explore your response to

---

Acceptance:

Have you felt a moment of acceptance of your parents' divorce?

How often do you find yourself in the place of acceptance?

If you were to place yourself between denial and acceptance on a continuum, where would you place yourself?

What has been or what is most helpful to you in finding the place of acceptance in the grieving process?

Shaken Foundations

the experience. Even when the moments of acceptance stretch into longer periods of resolution, there is still a tie to the divorce experience.

- Letting go happens when the picture of your life is not framed by the experience of your parents' divorce.
- Letting go happens when everything (or most of) what you think and feel is not related to the process of dealing with your parents' divorce and you begin to look at your own life and its choices.
- Letting go happens when dwelling in the process of a divorce opens up into the larger encounter with life.
- Letting go happens when your parents' divorce becomes integrated into the rest of your life story, when it is part of your story—but not the whole story.

In letting go, we let go of the past and become open to the possibilities of the future. Make a fist as if you were holding onto something tightly. Now slowly open your hand. You have moved from grasping to letting go. You can tell when you are still holding onto the experience of your parents' divorce when you feel emotionally, mentally, spiritually—or even physically—like that clenched fist. You can tell when you are letting go when you feel more like the open hand, ready to receive something new for your life.

The Bible talks a lot about hearts that are hardened. "Do not harden your hearts" (Psalm 95:8; Hebrews 3:8,15; 4:7). The people of God hardened their hearts when they were wandering in the wilderness. Because of this they were unable to hear the words and wisdom of God for their lives. They were unable to hope for the future or envision the new things of God for their lives. Hardened hearts are often spoken of in relation not only to the people cutting themselves off from God, but also cutting themselves off from each other. Hardened hearts often led to shunning others in need or to other acts of violence against members of the community.

Going through the process of your parents' divorce, doing the work of grieving, can feel like wandering in the wilderness where there is little sense of direction. The comforts of a former life are not available and neither are the promises of a new life. Even if life before your parents' divorce was not totally wonderful, you may (as in the case of God's people who left the horrors of being slaves in Egypt) still long for some of the security, certainty, or other small goodness it provided. Without *letting go* of the past, your own heart may be hardened toward the future. You may not be able to trust the power of God to bring life out of death, love out of hate, goodness out of what feels terrible in the present moment.

Sometimes letting go happens quite naturally. Sometimes it weaves itself into the grieving process and it is impossible to point to the place the grieving process stops and letting go begins. Sometimes letting go takes a little—or a lot—more work. Sometimes the past can hang around and haunt us. Sometimes it can keep popping up at the oddest and often most inopportune

Shaken Foundations

moments. Sometimes it requires a discipline of spirit that intentionally practices letting go.

When you have grieved what is lost and let it go, finding a new future and designing your life in a new way becomes possible.

Lost and Found

If I Could Read One Book . . .

Heart of Healing, Heart of Light: Encountering God, Who Shares and Heals Our Pain, Flora Slosson Wuellner. Wuellner offers guided meditations for emotional and spiritual healing.

For Your Reflection:

If you think about the stages or rooms of the grieving process, where do you think you are right now?

What other rooms have you visited?

How are you feeling about the grieving process overall?

What is the state of your heart in regard to your parents' divorce? Does it feel like a clenched fist, an open hand, or somewhere in between?

If you find yourself ready to let go, do you find it is happening naturally, or is it requiring some dedicated time, energy, and attentiveness from you?

Forgiveness and Reconciliation

> "Forgiveness is an essential part of the relational process by which hurts can be resolved, reconciliation achieved, and trust and mutual respect restored . . . Deciding to choose the option of forgiveness when we are hurt opens from our side the possibility for the injuries we suffer to be resolved into reconciliation."[1]
>
> —The Reverend Gregg Dana

Forgiveness. Reconciliation. Let's think about forgiveness and reconciliation. No, not between your parents, though they may work on this with each other at some point as well, or they may not. That is their business. Let's think about how you may need to forgive and to reconcile with others as a result of your parents' divorce. This is an important part of your own journey toward healing and wholeness.

When we recommend forgiveness and reconciliation as a part of healing, it is not just spiritual, emotional, or mental health about which we speak. New research is being done that suggests that it also is physically healthier to forgive than to carry a grudge. It is healthier to get in touch with your anger, make a choice to forgive, focus on the process of forgiveness, and find the freedom to move on with life that real forgiveness brings. Robert D. Enright at the University of Wisconsin began the research in the 1980s. Since then, there has been a lot of interest in "forgiveness studies." One study, at Hope College in Holland, Michigan, looked at the relationship between forgiveness and physical health. It was found that dwelling on feelings of revenge affected the cardiovascular system in a negatively stressful way. They also found that focusing on forgiveness caused the least amount of cardiovascular distress. Forgiveness is good for your soul *and* your body!

What is forgiveness? Forgiveness is the willingness to give up feelings of resentment that harden your heart. Forgiveness is the willingness to stop the running plots for revenge that go round and round in your head. Forgiveness is the willingness to reduce and finally do away with your resistance to someone who has injured you. Forgiveness is the willingness to let go of the urge toward retaliatory responses to get even with someone who has hurt you. It entails not just giving up the negative emotions toward someone with whom you have a legitimate

---

1. Gregg Dana, "Forgiveness," in *The Advocate*, January 2003, pp. 1–2.

Shaken Foundations

complaint, but also transforming those negative impulses into positive emotions and responses. Forgiveness is not just about taking out the trash in a relationship, but also picking some flowers from the garden as you come back in the door. Compassion, genuine concern for the one who has offended or hurt you, even hoping for good for that person, replace thoughts of revenge with actions for their well-being.

What forgiveness is not. Forgiveness is not forgetting. Whatever has happened to you, as a prelude to or as a result of your parents' divorce, is part of your story. It lives in your body and your soul whether you acknowledge it or not, whether you are aware of it or not, whether you want it to or not. Forgiveness does not mean denying your experience. It means working through your responses to that experience so that you remember it in a new way that frees you from its constraints on your happiness and creativity, in a way that frees you for shaping a healthy future for yourself.

Forgiveness is not making excuses for people. Forgiveness is not making up reasons why someone made bad decisions or acted irresponsibly. Forgiveness is not condoning inappropriate or injurious behavior. Forgiveness always begins with acknowledging that something wrong has been done.

Forgiveness is not a pardon for someone who has acted unwisely or destructively. Legally, a pardon is granted by a third party and affects a deserved punishment for an offending act.

Forgiveness and Reconciliation

Forgiveness is always a choice made by the one who was hurt by that act.

Forgiveness is not reconciliation. Forgiveness can be practiced and come to fruition without the offending person's participation. You can practice forgiveness and experience the release from the bondage of revenge without the other person's being involved. Reconciliation, however, requires the cooperation of the one who injured you. It is a mutual process of restoring that includes forgiveness and goes beyond it to rebuild the relationship on new ground.

Forgiveness is a spiritual discipline. When the disciples asked Jesus how many times they needed to forgive, he told them "seventy times seven." Jesus was suggesting to them that learning forgiveness is not a matter of mastering a formula. It is not a mechanical process. It is born of a true willingness for one's own transformation, for a move from deep negativity to lightness and openness of heart. It is making the journey of learning to love beyond liking, even to the point of loving one's enemies. This kind of loving is not about affectional bonds, but about knowing that at the beginning and the end of everything, of the whole world, there is a unity of which we are all a part. We all dwell in the circle of God's love. We are in relationship with one another, whether we like it or not, whether we like each other or not.

SHAKEN FOUNDATIONS

FORGIVENESS AND RECONCILIATION

> Think about what has happened in the course of your parents' divorce, to you and to your family. Are there people whom you feel you need to forgive?

Do you find yourself with a knot in your stomach when you are in the presence of one of your parents or someone else whom you hold responsible for their divorce?

Do you find you have feelings of revenge that swirl around in you?

Do you feel the flush of anger and resentment and urge to retaliate when you think about a person or a scenario related to the divorce?

Do you blame one or both of your parents for the divorce?

Was your relationship with one of them difficult or painful before their divorce? Has one of your parents hurt the other, and so hurt you?

Is there someone else involved in the divorce proceeding that you are holding responsible for the pain the divorce has caused? A family member? A friend of the family? Someone else?

As a result of the divorce, have you had fights or felt hurt by a sister or brother, or a member of your extended family?

As a result of the divorce, have you done things you wish you hadn't done that have hurt your parents or siblings or other family members? Sometimes it is yourself who is in need of forgiveness.

Shaken Foundations

Forgiving one another is learning to love largely as God loves us. Loving largely is healthier than hating. Forgiveness is healthier than resentment and retaliation.

In *Forgiveness Is a Choice: A Step by Step Process for Resolving Anger and Restoring Hope*, Robert Enright has identified four phases to forgiveness:

Phase One—Acknowledging Your Anger

This involves looking at your anger and how you deal with it. It includes looking at how much hold your anger has on you.

How much time, energy, and attention are you spending rehashing the situation? How much do you feel like lashing out at the particular person with whom you are angry? Do you have a lot of "displaced anger," anger at things other than the person who hurt you? The movement here is from a narrow focus on the pain to the ways it has changed your life.

Phase Two—Choosing to Forgive

After looking your anger square in the face and discovering that the way you have been dealing with it has not served you well, you can choose another course of attitude and action.

Phase Three—Focusing on Forgiveness

Forgiveness is hard work. Often it is helpful to have the aid of a professional counselor, pastor, or spiritual guide to walk with

Forgiveness and Reconciliation

you through this process. In this phase you will begin to accept the pain you are feeling and integrate it into your life story rather than continuing to lash out at others because of it. In doing this you both acknowledge the reality of pain and that it will not just disappear from your life. Know that you are empowered to reshape its effects on you, to learn from it, to gain wisdom from it and from your growth in love, as you begin to act compassionately both toward yourself and to the one who caused the pain.

Phase Four—Release from Bondage

In this phase, you may discover meaning in the midst of suffering and your own need to be forgiven for things you have done. You may come to understand more fully that you are not alone on this journey or any part of the journey of life. You may find true freedom from the poisons of fear, anger, resentment, hatred.[2]

To make this journey is to learn the true power of the Christian story. It is to be willing to experience death in order that new life may happen. In dying to your fear, anger, resentment, hostility, hatred, and urges for revenge and retaliation, you are free to start over, to begin again, to reshape your life, to write your own story without being limited by the effect other people's choices have had on your life.

Reconciliation moves beyond forgiveness to a mutual process of repairing the brokenness in relationship. Because

---

2. Cited by Alan Tripp, "To Forgive Is More Than Divine," in *Church of the Brethren Messenger*, July 2003, p. 17.

Forgiveness and Reconciliation

it requires the willingness of both parties, it may or may not be possible. You may invite someone to seek reconciliation with you, but she or he may not be ready to engage in the work of reconciliation with you. Your parents' divorce may divide you from a sibling as well as from a parent, from grandparents, from aunts and uncles, cousins, and from family friends. You may be willing to seek reconciliation, to repair relationships, but the other person may not be ready to work with you.

As with forgiveness, reconciliation is hard work. It requires the ability to tell the truth about what happened, to engage in forgiveness without clouding the truth or denying it, and to carefully rebuild relationships in a way that is mutually acceptable and healthy. This is a hard thing to do. Al Wynn, a former moderator of the Presbyterian Church (U.S.A.) reflects on the verse from Paul's letter to the Ephesians that talks of "speaking the truth in love" (4:15). Wynn reminds us that while speaking the truth is not hard, we can speak the truth in a way that is not loving. We can tell the truth in a way that not only does *nor* heal the wounds but that actually deepens them. He notes that loving is not hard if we are not willing to make waves by telling the truth to someone. But, he says, "speaking the truth in love" is very difficult. It requires that we find a way to tell the truth without sugarcoating it, but in a way that respects the other person and moves toward rebuilding a relationship with him or her. There is no reconciliation until the truth is told and both parties are able to acknowledge the truth

---

Shaken Foundations

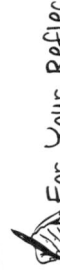

For Your Reflection:

If you have identified one or more people whom you want to forgive, where do you find yourself in the process of forgiveness with each of them?

Is there something for which you need to be forgiven?

Is there someone from whom you need to seek and receive forgiveness?

Shaken Foundations

about what has happened in their relationship. Then there must be a willingness to work to heal the wounds and move forward. To do all this, those involved must be assured that it is safe to engage in this truth telling. The assistance of a professional counselor, pastor, or spiritual guide is helpful in creating a safe space for this to happen.

The prophet Isaiah spoke of God's people being repairers of the breach (58:12), ones whose orientation is to mend what is broken in the world, especially in human relationships. He said this is the true worship in which God delights. Jesus spoke of loving even our enemies. In his letters to the early church, the apostle Paul spoke of the followers of Jesus as agents of reconciliation (2 Corinthians 5:18–19). We may think that these words refer to big things like working for world peace. And they do. The way we learn to work for world peace is to learn how to make peace in our own lives, in our homes, in our families, among our friends, in our local communities. When we work on reconciling relationships that have been broken as a consequence of divorce, we are rebuilding the most basic structure of community. We become peacemakers in our own families and learn skills for peacemaking in the larger world. Repairing the breach between your parents may not be possible, but repairing the brokenness in your relationship with each of them, with sisters and brothers, with other family members and friends, becomes a responsible act of adulthood, a choice for life-giving healing, even in the midst of what has been destroyed.

📖 If I Could Read One Book . . .

Don't Forgive Too Soon: Extending the Two Hands that Heal, by Dennis Linn, Sheila Fabricant Linn, and Matthew Linn

Or

Forgiveness Is a Choice: A Step by Step Process for Resolving Anger and Restoring Hope, by Robert Enright

Or

The Art of Forgiving, by Lewis Smedes

For Your Reflection:

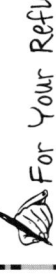

Think first about your parents and your relationships with them. Is there a need for reconciliation with either of them?

Think now of your immediate family—brothers or sisters, other close relatives. Is there a need for reconciliation with any of them?

Think about other people in your life with whom you may feel distance or brokenness in the relationship as a consequence, either direct or indirect, of your parents' divorce. With whom do you sense reconciliation is possible at this time?

If there is more than one person with whom you would seek reconciliation, with whom would you begin?

What do you think is the cause of the break in relationship?

What do you think the other person would say is the cause of the break in relationship?

What would you need to do to begin the process of reconciliation with this person?

What would hold you back from doing this?

What and who could and would support you in doing this?

Figuring Out Family Gatherings

holidays, graduations, weddings, and other occasions

> "Divorce . . . does not bring an end to the family."[1]
> —Ross A. Thompson, Paul R. Armato

Your parents divorced. Your parents may remain single after their divorce. Your parents may choose new partners. One parent may remain single. New partners may come into the relationship without children. New partners may already have children of their own. Your parent and the new partner may choose to have children together.

Your parents' divorce changes your family, but it does not end your family relationships. Your parents will always be your parents, whether or not they are actively a part of your life. If you have had siblings, they will always be your siblings, whether or not you are living with them. You may get along better with one parent than the other—before or after a divorce. You may get along with your siblings, or not, before or after a divorce. You may get along with your father's new spouse, but not your mother's new spouse. You may get along with neither or both. The same is true for step-siblings. Your new family may feel more comfortable than the old one. Your old family may have felt just fine and the new one may always feel awkward. Whatever happens after the divorce, you still have relationships with both your parents and their families. You also have relationships with any new people who become related to them. Figuring out how to relate to them is your choice, including whether you actively relate to them at all. This will include thinking about how you will relate to your family at holidays and special occasions throughout your life.

One of the lost items for children of divorce is the experience of parents as a couple for holidays, birthdays, graduations, vacations, and other family occasions. In addition to this loss, there may be pressure to be with one or the other parent at these times. You have the power to choose, to

---

1. Ross A. Thompson and Paul R. Armato, "The Postdivorce Family: An Introduction to the Issues," *The Postdivorce Family: Children, Parenting, and Society*, Ross A. Thompson and Paul R. Armato, eds. (Thousand Oaks, CA: Sage Publications, Inc., 1999), p. xi.

negotiate, to design, to create new traditions and new patterns for your celebration. You can decide how and where and when your parents will now be involved in your life. It may be very helpful if you have siblings to agree on what you want to happen so that you can support each other in your decisions.

Holidays

"The more importance your family has attached to holidays and the more elaborate your preparations have been, the harder it will be to break traditions and make drastic changes."[2]

"The holidays and weekends turned into days dissected into hours claimed by each parent."[3]

Three of the major challenges for holidays are named in these quotations: *what* will be done, *when* it will be done, and *with whom* it will be done.

What. Some families have elaborate rituals associated with holidays, repeated every year without significant variance. Other families simply enjoy the holidays as times for being together without adding a lot of extras to the daily routine. In either case, the absence of one parent, the move to a different house if that is part of the financial settlement in the divorce, the need to be with both parents at holiday time, or any number of other changes mean that what has been usual may no longer be so. While initially there may be an attempt to continue the familiar elements of celebration as a means of comfort or assurance, some change is often necessary and appropriate. You cannot alter the reason for the change, but you can creatively choose what changes you will make.

Perhaps the most important element in approaching the necessary changes is communication. Five steps to good communication about holidays (this goes for birthdays, too):

1. Know what has been important to you about your holiday celebrations in the past and why.
2. Acknowledge that things are different and that there will need to be some recognition of that in the way holidays are celebrated.
3. Together with the people with whom you will be celebrating, decide what you can and want to retain and what may need to be revised.
4. After the holiday, talk about how it felt. Honestly. What worked? What didn't work? Remember the first time through something new or unfamiliar, the new way won't feel the same way the old way did so you may want to give it another chance.
5. Be willing to make further revisions.

Honesty in this process is very important. Your mother may think she is doing you a favor by keeping things as close to the way they were as possible. If you don't tell her that you would prefer to try something new, she will never know. Chad

---

2. Vicki Lansky, *Divorce Book for Parents: Helping Your Children Cope with Divorce and Its Aftermath* (New York: New American Library, 1989), p. 210.
3. Stephanie Staal, *The Love They Lost: Living with the Legacy of Our Parents' Divorce* (New York: Delacorte Press, 2000), p. 16.

Shaken Foundations

told us that this was the hardest part of the first holiday after his parents' divorce. Both parents were present for the Thanksgiving holiday. Things were made to feel "normal" when they weren't. This was more painful for Chad than acknowledging that life and "home" had changed forever and beginning to deal with the changes.

If your father thinks he needs to duplicate or compete with what your mother is doing and this creates a tension for you that only makes things worse, it may be helpful to let him know how you feel. Again, it is important for you to sort out what you need and understand what others need and negotiate what is good for all of you. You may want to ask yourself, "What makes a holiday a 'special' day? What makes the celebration healthy and honors the event being celebrated?"

It is also important to remember that things take time. Phillip, whose parents divorced when he was in his twenties, said it took four years for his family to get in sync with holidays. **When and With Whom**. The "when" and "with whom" questions may feel like a tug of war contest with you as the rope. If your parents live in the same city, both may expect you to be with them on the holidays. If they live in different cities they may expect you to alternate years. One young adult suggests that it is very important to protect your own time. While remembering that you are not the only one involved in the decision, and that we all live in relationship with one

Figuring Out Family Gatherings

another, think through on how you want to spend your holidays, your birthday, your vacation. How will you share the time you have without wearing yourself out or alienating one or both parents? Consider that one year it may be possible to see everyone and in other years you may not be able to do that.

Ellen, whose parents divorced when she was in college, found going home at holiday time to be very difficult. She always felt torn between her parents' houses, neither of which felt like home to her. She decided that when she went home, she would stay at a motel. She would see each parent for a few hours but not stay at either one's home.

Alice spent her childhood years tossed back and forth between parents who were always in conflict. In her young adult years, she decided to do holidays differently. "My goal is to start having holidays at my house—and whoever wants to come is welcome. That's the way I'm going to do it, and I feel pretty strongly about it . . . I'm tired of bouncing around. There have been losses along the way. I definitely never had the feeling of 'I'm home, and everyone is here and everything is right in the world.' I make visits, but they are more like targeted hits."[4]

Because these women were in touch with their own feelings and needs, they were able to articulate what they wanted and to create an alternative.

---

4. Stephanie Staal, *The Love They Lost: Living with the Legacy of Our Parents' Divorce* (New York: Delacorte Press, 2000), p. 220.

SHAKEN FOUNDATIONS

However you decide to meet the challenge of "when and with whom" at holidays, communicating clearly what you are doing and why is important. Your parents and family may understand and support you in your decision, especially if you have laid out the reasons and included them in the conversation and in seeking a good solution for all parties. On the other hand, even if you communicate your own needs well and make reasonable, creative, and good suggestions about resolving the issues, one or both of your parents may not understand or support your decision. You still have the responsibility to communicate clearly and be willing to negotiate compromise if that is possible. Even if they are not willing to act as adults, you can!

FIGURING OUT FAMILY GATHERINGS

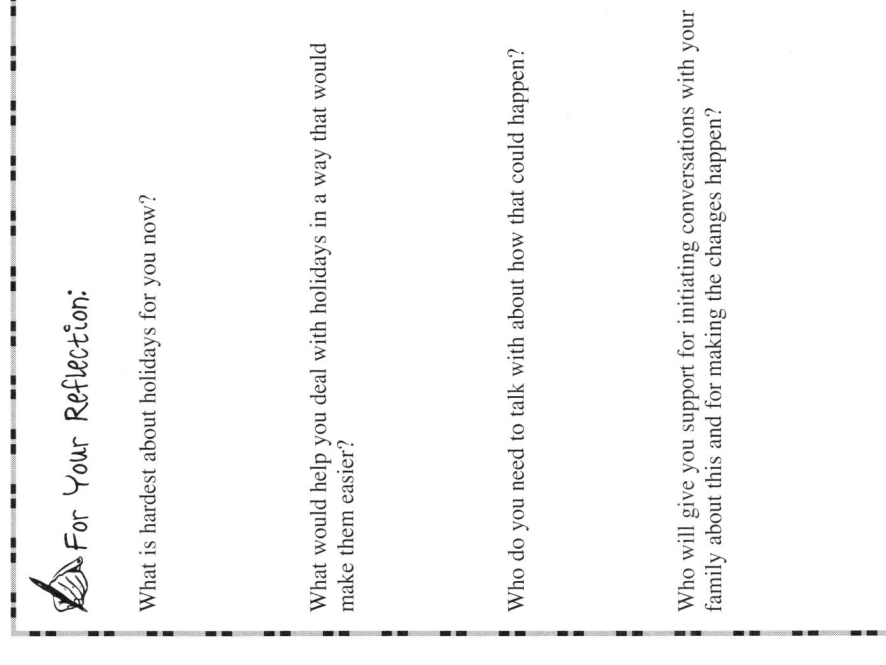

For Your Reflection:

What is hardest about holidays for you now?

What would help you deal with holidays in a way that would make them easier?

Who do you need to talk with about how that could happen?

Who will give you support for initiating conversations with your family about this and for making the changes happen?

Public and Semi-public Occasions

"... The mere thought of having them in the same room tense and silent sent me into a panic."[1]

—Stephanie Staal

Graduation. Entering public service. An award for volunteering in the community. Recognition of achievement at work. Your family may be invited to participate in any such occasions—in public. This may be fine, easy, or no problem if your parents' divorce was a mutual agreement. However, if your parents did not divorce amicably, or if one parent did not want the divorce, having them both at such occasions may take some creative thinking and planning on your part.

Rachel thought through the scenario of her college graduation and decided to count on the best and plan for the worst. She got together with several of her friends whose parents were also divorced and reserved a room at a local restaurant with several tables in it. All the parents were invited. As long as they "behaved themselves" they would sit at the table with their graduate. If anything threatened to interrupt the celebration, there was a plan for the parents to be separated so that former spouses would not sit together but with other parents. As it turned out, everyone behaved and had a good time, but the plan was there—just in case.

Life Passages: Weddings, Baptisms, Funerals

"At [Alice's] wedding, she is insisting that both her parents sit together at her table. 'I think if I had gotten married five years ago, I would have had separate tables, but now I feel like, you know, this is my deal. I've had to adjust my schedule to their schedules and agendas for a long time, and for one day, everyone is going to be happy for us. That's how it's going to be.' She smiles and then concludes, 'It took a lot of work for me to get to that level.'"[2]

There will be other significant events in your life at which family and friends may gather. They will also be public in that

---

1. Stephanie Staal, *The Love They Lost: Living with the Legacy of Our Parents' Divorce* (New York: Delacorte Press, 2000), p. 17.
2. Stephanie Staal, *The Love They Lost: Living with the Legacy of Our Parents' Divorce* (New York: Delacorte Press, 2000), p. 220.

PUBLIC AND SEMI-PUBLIC OCCASIONS

they will usually happen outside your own home space and may include people whom you do not know. They may be events over which you do not have total control. You may not even be in charge. However, as a primary participant, you will have an influence on what happens and how it happens. It is important to think ahead to these events, to think about what you want to happen, to identify with whom you want to share the occasion, to consider the potential problems and the potential solutions. How do you deal with the family gathering at (a) your wedding, a happy celebration; (b) at your baby's baptism, a sacred moment; and (c) at the memorial service of a dear family friend, a sad occasion?

For some people, their parents have done their own homework and have creatively worked through the things that separated them so that they can be together at these events. Each of them has gone on with their lives and is able to be supportive of you as you go on with yours.

For other people, the presence of both parents at any gathering is enormously difficult and produces an uncertainty or anxiety that clouds the occasion, dulling its joy or complicating its sorrow. If you find yourself in this group, it is important to assess your own needs, think through the situation and the possibilities for both what could go right and what could go wrong, plan ahead, articulate alternatives, and negotiate agreements about acceptable behavior.

SHAKEN FOUNDATIONS

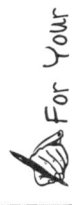

For Your Reflection:

Generally, how do you assess your parents' ability to get along at a public occasion? (Civility and good manners are the standard here.)

What occasions do you foresee in the near or far future when there may need to be some accommodation for your parents due to their divorce?

How will you plan for that event?

Do you have friends with whom you can consult about this?

Shaken Foundations

Rebecca and Brad worked hard on their wedding plans, including thinking through how to deal with their four parents, each of whom had a new partner. When it came time for the parents of the bride and groom to bless the couple, the pastor invited each of Brad's and Rebecca's parents to stand, naming them along with the new spouse. Eight people responded to the question "Who comes to bless this marriage?" Their resounding "We do" was both a testimony to the good forethought on the part of the groom and bride and a healthy indication that there would be ample parental support for this couple as they designed their own marriage and made the journey through life together.

Phillip offers his own experience: "I have found that in our family, an important thing has been to have each person in the family make up their own rules as to how to handle the situation. I, for instance, explicitly told my father that he could not bring his wife to my wedding. That helped me feel empowered and to draw lines around family time that I needed to call my own."[3]

Thinking about situations such as these in advance, establishing boundaries, negotiating compromises, and communicating expectations are important in dealing creatively with family occasions that may be made difficult because of your parents' divorce. Rachel and Phillip dealt with their wedding celebrations in different ways. Each, however, thought through the event ahead of time and set a plan in place to deal with possible problems.

Public and Semi-public Occasions

As we acknowledged at the beginning of this section, divorce does not erase family ties. Questions of how to deal with family relationships will be present throughout your life and theirs. Over the years, some of the issues may be resolved through hard work or eased with time. Sometimes bitterness remains, and dealing thoughtfully, creatively, and compassionately with family members will reduce the prospect of the worst that can happen and increase the possibility of the best that can happen for everyone.

Sometimes, no matter how much you think ahead, no matter how well you plan, things do not go as well as you had hoped. You may find yourself caught in the middle. Here are some things to remember and do if that happens:

- Breathe. Acknowledge what is happening and breathe through it. Taking a deep breath allows you a moment to gather up your own spiritual resources to meet the situation and to choose to respond creatively rather than merely react in a way that may only make the situation worse. Breathing deeply puts you in touch with the presence of God in any particular situation and is a reminder that you are not alone in facing what is happening.
- Remember that you are living your story, not your parents' story. You have the creative power to model healthy behavior for them. By behaving as an adult,

---

3. Quotes from author's questionnaire to young adults whose parents have divorced.

you may assist them in doing so as well. If they are not willing or able to cooperate, you also have the creative power to ask that they leave the event so that others may enjoy or observe the reason for the gathering. You may need to enlist help with this from someone else who is present such as the pastor or a family friend who knows one or both of your parents well. Asking for help in such a situation is appropriate.

- Remember that you have choices about how you respond to whatever is going on. You are not able to choose how you feel about what is happening. It may even evoke some old and familiar feelings with which you thought you had dealt long ago. However, in the present, you can choose how you will respond. That is part of writing your own story, rather than living as an extension of your parents' story.

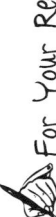 IF I COULD READ ONE BOOK . . . .

The Love They Lost: Living with the Legacy of Our Parents' Divorce by Stephanie Staal deals with issues related to the whole experience of life after one's parents' divorce and contains specific material related to dealing with holidays and other public family occasions.

For Your Reflection:

As you think about the celebratory and solemn occasions of life, what kind of parental presence and support do you want and anticipate?

What work do you need to do right now to prepare for an event in the future—your wedding, a baptism, your child's school play or soccer match, a significant anniversary party, a major surgery, a memorial service—where both parents, and perhaps their partners, will be present?

What will you need to do in the future to plan well for healthy outcomes for family gatherings on important occasions?

What boundaries will you set?

How will you seek the cooperation of your parents, and perhaps their spouses, in shaping an event that honors your own needs and respects theirs?

Designing Your Own Relationship

"If you don't marry, you don't get betrayed. You don't divorce. You're safe from a whole lot of things. That's reality. I'm in my thirties and I've never been in love where I felt like somebody was the right person and that I'm going to spend the rest of my life with him. People say you just know it if you're in love. I've never known it and I doubt I ever will. I've pretty much been convinced my whole life that I'm not going to have a romantic relationship that works. I'm sure I'm not the first to tell you that."[1]

—"Lisa," quoted by Judith Wallerstein, Julia Lewis, and Sandra Blakeslee

Judith Wallerstein found that about forty percent of the men and women in her study on children of divorce never married. That percentage was higher than the national average for those who had grown up in families that did not experience divorce.

Fear of commitment, or more accurately, the fear of a broken commitment, was at the core of most of the reasons for not marrying. Because of their own history and the divorce culture in which they grew up, many were afraid to enter into significant committed relationships. There was a strong sense of distrust that the marriage bonds would last. There was a belief that if they cohabitated with someone it was easier to get out and move on with life than with a legalized marriage relationship.

There is another story, though.

Robert Emery's research finds that in spite of an increased risk for a variety of difficulties in immediate adjustment and in later life, "*resilience* is the normative outcome of divorce for children . . ."[2] He notes that while there is significant psychological pain, it more often manifests itself as distress than dysfunction. He says: ". . . the wounds of most children heal; but even healed wounds leave a scar."[3] Resilience and healing offer hope that children of divorced parents may deal creatively with their own lives. Aware of their own scars, they

---

1. Judith Wallerstein, Julia Lewis, and Sandra Blakeslee, *The Unexpected Legacy of Divorce: A 25 Year Landmark Study* (New York: Hyperion, 2000), p. 289.
2. Robert Emery, "Postdivorce Family Life for Children," *The Postdivorce Family: Children, Parenting, and Society*, Ross A. Thompson and Paul R. Armato, eds., (Thousand Oaks, CA: Sage Publications, 1999), p. 4.
3. Robert Emery, "Postdivorce Family Life for Children," *The Postdivorce Family: Children, Parenting, and Society*, Ross A. Thompson and Paul R. Armato, eds., (Thousand Oaks, CA: Sage Publications, 1999), p. 18.

Shaken Foundations

can design a different way of being in a relationship and can succeed in marriage even though their parents failed.

When asked if her parents' divorce had made any difference in her own life, Margaret said, "Maybe it makes me work harder at my own relationship." An alternative response to the story of your parents' divorce is to learn what makes for a healthy relationship and to pursue that as a priority in your life.

Designing Your Own Relationship

The marriage you know best, for good or for ill, is that of your own parents. That is true whether it is a good marriage or a bad marriage, a marriage that lasts or one that ends in separation or divorce.

Whether or not you are aware of it, you have learned a lot about marriage from your parents. Much of that is not conscious learning. It may have seeped in over the years and formed expectations in you or patterns in your behavior that you may not be able to articulate at this moment. Or perhaps you have done a lot of thinking about and analyzing of your parents' marriage, and, perhaps, their divorce. Whatever your experience, the most important thing to remember as you consider your own ability to form a relationship, grow in that relationship, commit to that relationship, and continue to care for that relationship throughout your life is that *you are not your parents*. You are a product of your parents' marriage either by birth or adoption. You have been influenced by their marriage patterns and their decision to divorce. But, *you have the power and ability to design your own relationship*. You are writing your own story now. You can decide and design your life and your relationship.

How do you design a relationship? We can't go into all there is to say about forming healthy relationships and tending a lifelong commitment. However, here are some suggestions to consider:

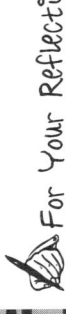 For Your Reflection:

Where do you find yourself right now?

Would you agree more with Lisa or Margaret?

Are you somewhere in the middle?

Where would you like to be?

Shaken Foundations

- *Know yourself.* Spend time. Do the work of getting to know your own patterns, preferences, and priorities, your wounds and vulnerabilities, your strengths and delights, your hopes and dreams, your moral values and spiritual experiences.
- *Know your partner.* Spend time. Do the work of getting to know him or her in the same way you have gotten to know yourself.
- *Reflect on your parents' marriage and divorce.* What was good about their marriage? What was not good? Why did it not work for either or both of them? Is there anything from their marriage that you want to make sure is part of your own relationship? Is there anything you definitely don't want to be part of yours?
- *Ask your partner to reflect on her or his parents' relationship, and divorce, if that is part of her or his history as well.* Find out what he or she would like to keep and what he or she would not want to keep as part of your relationship.
- *Assess where you are in your own healing process in regard to your parents' divorce.* Are there still open wounds? What are the scars you continue to bear from their divorce? How do those affect your everyday living and, particularly, how you function in a relationship? Are there situations or behaviors of which you need to be

Designing Your Own Relationship

acutely aware because they can reopen places of hurt? Share these with your partner.

- *Talk. Talk. Talk. Talk some more.* Learn good interpersonal communication skills if you don't have them already. Talk to your partner about your past, your present, and your future. Ask about your partner's past, present, and future. Talk about your deepest fears and your dearest hopes.
- *Find a good counselor.* If you are considering making a life commitment to someone, find someone who specializes in helping couples think about the issues of long-term commitment in a relationship. If you are married, find someone who specializes in helping couples look at what is happening in their relationship. It is often helpful to have the assistance of a third party in talking about especially difficult topics or already conflicted topics.
- *Find mentors.* In spite of all the statistics about divorce, there are some very faithful, creative, intimate, and nourishing relationships. Find a couple with a healthy relationship. Ask them if they would be willing to be your mentors. Have a meal with them on a regular basis and talk with them about what their relationship is like and how they work to keep the relationship healthy. Ask how they deal with conflict, difficult life events,

disappointments. Ask them how they celebrate their anniversaries and how they decided what they would do on holidays or birthdays. Ask how they have agreed to get the bills paid, do the laundry, mow the lawn, buy the groceries, and deal with each other's families. Your mentors' relationship is a good model, but this does not mean you must replicate their relationship. These conversations are to help you think about how you want to make decisions in your own relationship.

- *Read*. Read a few well-recommended books on relationships and marriage. You will find some listed in the bibliography. Read at least one of them together and talk about it with one another.
- *Develop some common agreements about what you want your relationship to look like*. This doesn't need to look like a contract, and it won't be static. Leave room for each of you to grow individually and for you to grow together as your relationship moves through the stages of life. Check in each year on how this is feeling to each of you on your anniversary or some other date upon which you decide together. Talk about what is and what is not working—and why that's the case. Make revisions to reflect new events (like children or school or job change or extended family issues).
- *Play*. Don't stop playing together. Some couples establish a "date night" each week to make sure they keep in touch with the things that brought them together. Laughter and play are healing and healthy for a relationship.
- *Community*. It has been said before. It bears saying again. God created the universe, the whole cosmos as a community. We belong to one another and we are intended to share life together, our sorrows, joys, challenges, celebrations. Find friends wherever you are with whom you can share the experience of growing and changing. Community is not just a geographic reality; it is also a spiritual reality. Don't forget old friends who knew you way back when. Keep in touch with family folks who are supportive of your lives and your life together. Consider keeping in touch with those people you invited to your wedding celebration. They were witnesses to your love for one another at that event and can be called upon to support you as your relationship deepens. If you are planning a wedding, think about including an explicit question to the congregation that asks them to support you beyond the wedding event.
- *Grow*. Individually and together. Keep growing. Keep yourself alive and active and available to life in all its fullness. Life is God's great gift to each of you and love is God's great gift to both of you. Keep growing in life and love.

This last suggestion about growth warrants some special attention.

Shaken Foundations

As we noted in the chapter titled "Dealing with Divorce," one of the consequences of growing up in a dysfunctional family environment may be some measure of arrested development. If your parents fought a lot, if there were alcohol or drug dependencies, or a lack of emotional intimacy, the process of becoming an adult, of maturing mentally, emotionally, and spiritually, may have gotten short-circuited. Coping mechanisms that were necessary for survival in a conflicted or otherwise dysfunctional family may be maintained long after the particular circumstances that evoked them have passed. They may impede the process of establishing your own life and relationships. Recognizing and growing beyond the mental, emotional, and spiritual patterns established to cope with your parents' divorce and the resulting family dynamics is an important step in growing beyond them, in growing up into mature adulthood.

David Richo has written a book called *How to Be an Adult*. In his focus on establishing intimacy and forming healthy relationships, he says: "A relationship is a spiritual path since it consists of a continual shedding of illusions."[4]

By this he means that being in relationship is part of the spiritual journey to honesty and wholeness, toward claiming our true self and living in community with others. This journey takes us not only into intimate relationship with others, but also into intimate relationship with ourselves as we come to terms with our history and as we move into our future. Being honest about the past that can't be changed and how it affected us, and being realistic about who we are and what we want and need for fullness of life means shedding illusions and giving up impossible fantasies. It means wrestling with the truth of our lives about both how bad and how good it has been. It means recognizing our woundedness and seeking healing. It means finding the courage to live beyond what has happened so that we can freely live differently for and with others.

Real intimacy with a life partner will not allow us to hide from ourselves or our partners. Real intimacy will expose us to the best and worst of ourselves as we live in the discipline of a relationship. Real intimacy will require us to be aware of ourselves and of how we behave. Real intimacy will support us in making changes to become more healthy and more whole. Richo rightly calls this a spiritual journey because it takes courage to do this, more than we can muster on our own. The courage to grow up, to change, to embrace life, is a gift of grace, a gift of God.

As you consider designing your relationship with a life partner, one of the things you may want to think about is how each of you experiences and relates to God, to the Sacred, to the Holy in life. How will God be part of your life together? At the close of some wedding services, there is a sentence that goes something like this: "What God has joined together, let no

---

4. David Richo, *How to Be an Adult: A Handbook on Psychological and Spiritual Integration* (Mahwah, NJ: Paulist Press, 1991), p. 85.

LIFE IN ABUNDANCE

In speaking of his own ministry, Jesus describes the purpose of his mission as bringing life, life in abundance. By this, he did not mean physical existence, not just breathing and a heartbeat. The life to which he referred is LIFE! The life that Jesus came to make possible is not limited to fulfillment of basic needs for water, food, and shelter. LIFE! is a fullness of life that includes trust, creativity, discovery, and celebration. It is vibrant and dynamic, expansive and willing to risk change for the better. God's intention for us is LIFE! in abundance: genuine love, overflowing joy, authentic community, and deep peace.

Sometimes life before a divorce has been unstable or violent. If life has felt untrustworthy, the experience of divorce may improve the immediate situation but without dealing with the leftovers of fear, anxiety, confusion, and insecurity. If your parents' divorce seems sudden or without reason, life can feel very uncertain. The world you knew best is altered and will never be the same. You may think: If this happened, what else can happen? Fear can override the faith that life holds great goodness and is worth investing in. Anxiety can cloud decisions or become a haunting companion. Violence done to us may become violence we do to others before violence is done to us again. Sometimes the pain and uncertainty become so overwhelming that death seems a more reasonable option than life.

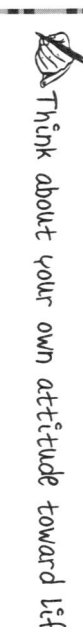

Think about your own attitude toward life.

On a continuum of 1 to 10 with 1 being "life"—shriveled, meager, sparse, painful, tight, cramped—and 10 being LIFE!—robust, active, engaged, eager, abundant, expansive—where would you put yourself?

life 1 2 3 4 5 6 7 8 9 10 LIFE!!!

What words would you use to describe your attitude toward life?

What words would you like to use to describe your attitude toward life?

What healing do you sense needs to happen for you to move from where you are now to where you would like to be?

Shaken Foundations

give love. This practice of love is not an either/or. It is a both/and. Selfishness is loving only yourself. Loving others without being able to receive love in return or without being able to love one's self is not real love. It tends toward manipulation. The kind of loving that Jesus describes is holistic loving that begins with God and flows with reciprocity in our relationships with friends, family, strangers, even enemies.

The experience of divorce has the potential for calling into question our certainty that we are loved. Abandonment, either physical or emotional, by one or both parents can block our awareness of being loved and inhibit our ability to love others, not only in romantic love, but also in friendship and family. The disruption in our parents' love for one another and the consequence of disruption in their love for us can lead to behaviors that lean either toward selfishness or manipulation, toward focusing only on our own lives or trying to change the world because we think it is impossible to change ourselves. It can also lead to isolation and fantasy life or to workaholism and an emphasis on producing something valuable to others so that we feel valuable and worthy ourselves.

Learning to love and be loved is at the heart of spiritual growth for all God's people. It holds particular challenges for children and young adults whose parents have divorced.

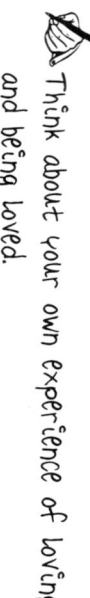

Think about your own experience of loving and being loved.

As you think about your parents' divorce, what effect has it had on your ability to love—self, others, God?

Does it seem more difficult to love others or does it seem more difficult to love yourself?

What would you identify as the challenges you face in learning to love yourself, your neighbor, and God?

What would you identify as the challenges you face in learning to be loved?

SPIRITUAL GROWTH

"You shall love the Lord your God with all your heart, and with all your soul, and with all your strength, and with all your mind; and your neighbor as yourself." —Luke 10:27

"I came that they may have life, and have it abundantly." —John 10:10

"So if anyone is in Christ, there is a new creation: everything old has passed away; see, everything has become new!" —2 Corinthians 5:17

"I have set before you life and death, blessings and curses. Choose life . . ." —Deuteronomy 30:19

There are many ways to talk about the spiritual life and the spiritual journey. There are many ways to describe spiritual growth and formation. The Scripture passages above represent four basic characteristics of spiritual life and growth that may be particularly important as you experience and work through your parents' divorce.

LOVE

In the passage from Luke, Jesus makes clear that love is central to our spiritual life and to the process of maturing in our relationship with God, self, and others.

Throughout the biblical witness, it is clear that God is the source of love, the source of all that is loving. God's creative energy is expressed in love and through love. God's redemptive activity holds love at its core. God's sustaining spirit supports us both in direct experience with the Sacred and by the supportive relationships around us that are manifestations of God's love in our lives.

God's intention for us is that we are all loved and that we will be loving in all our relationships with each other. The greatest challenge in life is love: to be loved and to love, to love oneself and to love our neighbors, to receive love and to

70

SHAKEN FOUNDATIONS

one tear apart." Another way of saying that might be, "Those who recognize God to be the source of their love have a strong spiritual support for their life together." God is a companion not only for your personal spiritual journey, but for your journey in marriage and family, in union with one another.

IF I COULD READ ONE BOOK . . .

To Love and Be Loved by Sam Keen offers deep reflections on love and commitment in relationships.

Or

How to Be an Adult: A Handbook on Psychological and Spiritual Integration by David Richo is a good overall book about maturing psychologically and spiritually. Chapter 8 specifically deals with intimacy in this process of maturing.

DESIGNING YOUR OWN RELATIONSHIP

For Your Reflection:

What are your fears about a committed relationship?

What are your hopes for a committed relationship?

What impediments do you see in your past and present to living in a committed relationship through the changes and challenges of life?

What resources do you see in yourself that will assist you in living in a committed relationship through the changes and challenges of life?

Who would you identify as a couple whom you see as having a good, healthy, creative, mutually supportive, and mature relationship?

What are the qualities of that relationship that you would like to have in your own relationship?

How do you see your relationship with God being a part of your designing your own committed relationship?

Shaken Foundations

Spiritual growth during difficult times includes (a) assessing where we are in relation to God's intention that our lives be abundant and joyful, (b) addressing the gap between where we find ourselves and the fullness of life Jesus showed to us, and (c) healing the wounds of heart, mind, and spirit that affect our ability to embrace life with eagerness and anticipation.

Life Is a Journey

Within the biblical witness, there are many images of movement, of leaving one place and moving to another, of leaving one circumstance and moving to another, of leaving one attitude and moving to another. The story of the Exodus is the story of movement from slavery to freedom. The story of Good Friday and Easter is the story of movement from death to resurrection/new life. Over and over again, the story of God's people is the story of movement from being asleep (or numb or ignorant) to being awake and aware and attuned to God's presence in the world and God's power at work in the world.

In the book of Hebrews, chapter 11, there is a long recitation of people who "made the journey" from one place to another, from one situation in life to another, from one way of seeing the world to a new understanding of themselves in relation to the world, their neighbors, and God. The author of Hebrews describes these people as people of faith. "Now faith is the assurance of things hoped for, the conviction of things not seen" (Hebrews 11:1). In order to make the spiritual journey, the people of God had to believe that the things for which they hoped — freedom, renewal, awareness — were not only possible, but already real in the vision and intent of God.

Faith and hope are essential to living life as a joyful journey. The experience of a family in which conflict is dealt with by verbal or physical violence, or in which mental, emotional, or physical illness (such as clinical depression or alcoholism) are present can erode faith and hope. Faith and hope can also be eroded in a family in which there is no expressed affection between parents and perhaps none toward their children or in which infidelity is either a shadowy party to the marriage or an explicit and acknowledged element in it. Cynicism is the opposite of faith and hope. It can become a constant buffer that grants space between our deep and dearest hopes for life and the reality we experience every day. Cynicism is a serious blockade to living life as a great adventure that leads to discovery of the self and the Sacred.

The spiritual journey invites us, then, to move from the places we have been enslaved by the past into a new place where freedom to live life fully is possible. It calls us to risk leaving the familiar patterns and behaviors we used to cope with difficult situations and to move to creative practices that promote health and wholeness. This isn't as easy as it sounds. When Moses led the people of God out of slavery in Egypt and into the wilderness on the forty-year journey to Canaan, the

Shaken Foundations

Promised Land, he found that the Hebrew people started to rebel against his leadership. They actually liked some things that had been part of their days as slaves. Even though slavery was a terrible thing for them, for their bodies and their spirits, they longed for familiar things. Canaan and the new life seemed a long way off and the journey seemed to take forever.

Leaving behind the hurt of the past in order to find hope for the future is not as easy as it sounds. The burden of a painful past is like any other kind of burden. If you have been carrying a heavy pail of water for a long distance, when you put it down, it will take a while for your hands to become flexible and supple again. They have become shaped or conformed to the handle of the pail and to the need to carry the heavy weight of the water. So it is with our spiritual, emotional, mental lives. If you have been carrying a heavy burden for a long time, you may have gotten used to it. You may have gotten so used to it that even after you put it down (after the immediate experience of it is over), you still act as if you were in it. It feels as if all of life is or will be like the difficult experience that shaped you by its weight of violence, isolation, loneliness, abuse, or other wounds to body and spirit.

Divorce can shape you in a way that affects you long beyond the experience itself. Making the journey from the places where you feel enslaved by that experience to a new place of freedom is part of your spiritual growth. Letting go

Spiritual Growth

of the past, "dying to the past and its ways" as prayers of confession often put it, is another way of thinking about this journey. In the course of our lives, we will go through many journeys of death and resurrection as we move from what no longer serves us to a new reality of life that enhances our ability to be fully who God created us to be. Jesus showed us that we need not fear this journey, that in the wisdom of God's great design, life is stronger than death. The power of resurrection is real. We can trust that God will bring us through the pain and suffering of our lives to healing and hope if we are willing to make the journey.

Sometimes we cope with difficulty by creating a fantasy life. The experience of your parents' divorce can invite you to the journey from being asleep to being awake, from fantasy to faithfulness.

Living a fantasy life may have many expressions. You may retreat into the world of television, movies, books, or your own thinking that creates an alternative to what is painful around you. If you live in this fantasy world, you isolate yourself from reality and you separate yourself from those who live in the real world. This is like being asleep or numb or ignorant of what is really happening. This may be a short-term escape or a long-term coping mechanism. Sometimes this pretend world may become the place in which we live for a long while. The spiritual journey calls us to wake up, to engage in life as it is, to deal with what is difficult and find creative alternatives to it.

74

Spiritual Growth

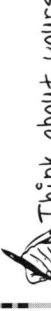 *Think about yourself right now.*

Which words in these pairs seem to fit your life most right now? Slavery or freedom? Death or resurrection/new life? Asleep or awake?

Can you name what it is that may be causing you to avoid dealing with the reality of your life?

Can you identify any fears that hold you back from moving toward a more creative, engaged, and active participation in your life?

Can you imagine what it would be like to wake up to life? What would be different? How would you be different?

What first step or next step would you need to take to continue your spiritual journey?

Shaken Foundations

Another expression of being asleep or numb or ignorant is that of optimism. Optimism in our culture sometimes sounds a lot like hope, but it is not like it at all. Optimism, like pessimism, is one-sided. Where pessimism says that nothing good can happen, optimism says that everything will be fine. It will all work out. Parents will reconcile. A scholarship will come. You will win the lottery or get the dream job. Prince or Princess Charming will arrive. Generally, the implication is that we don't have to do anything to assist what happening. Hope, on the other hand, acknowledges that even though some things are not right, the possibility exists that new things can come out of the present difficulty. Here is that death and resurrection journey again! Out of the worst winter, spring can come. Out of death, new life springs forth. We can count on these patterns as part of God's great design, but we must wake up to notice them and then participate in making them happen. The spiritual journey leads us to look at life honestly and acknowledge the truth about where we are, then to move with hope through the present to a different, more creative future.

The Freedom to Choose

One of the most difficult awarenesses of the spiritual life is that we have the freedom to choose. From the beginning, choice is central to God's relationship with humanity. Adam and Eve, Cain and Abel, Jacob and Esau, Moses, Jonah, Mary, the many men and women we know as the disciples of Jesus, Pilate, the apostle Paul, all of these people made significant life choices. Jesus himself had to choose between good and evil in the desert as the Adversary placed temptations before him, and again in the Garden of Gethsemane, and in many situations in between. In the book of Deuteronomy, the situation is made clear. God has designed the universe in such a way that we are given the freedom to choose how we will live. We can choose life and prosperity or death and adversity. We can choose blessings or curses (Deuteronomy 30:19). We can choose to "go with God" or not. We can choose to ask "What would Jesus do?" or not. We can choose to do God's thing or our own thing without considering God's thing at all.

God has given us freedom and called us to be responsible in it—able to respond to life as it happens. And life *will* happen. Good times happen. Bad times happen. Marriage happens. Divorce happens. God does not give us guarantees that life will be all roses. There's a better chance that if we "go with God," the choices we make will lead us to good things. There's an excellent chance that if we choose to be selfish or ignorant, vengeful or stupid, or do drugs or engage in promiscuous behavior, we will experience "curses" (very negative consequences).

SHAKEN FOUNDATIONS

SPIRITUAL GROWTH

> Think about the choices you have already made in response to your parents' divorce.

Would you say that most of the choices you have made have been life-giving choices?

Can you identify a choice that you have made that was not a life-giving choice?

How did that feel as you made it?

Can you identify any adverse consequences that have come from this? Adverse consequences mean more than getting caught or punished for illegal or even unwise behavior. They may be deeper results of our choices that leave long-term residues of regret, self-doubt, or sadness.

Can you identify one choice you have made that you would call life-giving? How did that feel as you made it?

What helps you choose life instead of death, blessing instead of curse?

Shaken Foundations

Though we can make choices about our own behavior, we cannot control the behavior of others. God has also created the universe to be a dynamic community so that what we do affects others and what others do affects us. If your parents divorce, you have no choice in the decision, but it will affect your life. And yet, you still are free to choose some things. You are free to choose how you will respond to their divorce. You are free to choose whether you will respond by punishing them for their decision or seeking to establish as good relationships with each of them as possible. You are free to choose how you will make healthy decisions for your own life given the decisions they have made in theirs (see "Figuring Out Family Gatherings"). You are free to choose whether you will let the fact that their marriage didn't work out influence whether you will marry and develop a healthy relationship or will never commit yourself to anyone (see "Designing Your Own Relationship").

One aspect of the spiritual journey is learning to deal with God's gift of freedom and learning to choose for health and wholeness. From that perspective, the whole point of this book is to encourage you to be free to choose, and to *choose life.*

Spiritual growth is as important in our lives as the growth of our bodies, the growth of our intellect, the growth of our emotional lives. Our growth in all these areas makes us whole people, healthy people. Throughout the life of God's people there have been particular disciplines, or exercises or practices that have helped people grow spiritually. Some of these are

Spiritual Growth

Bible study, prayer, guided meditation, journaling, contemplative silence, and spiritual guidance. Some of these have been suggested throughout this book. Other resources are listed below. Spiritual disciplines are not just for a time of crisis. They are intended as ways to help us all along the journey of life so that our spiritual dimension may deepen and be shaped by our growing relationship with God.

📖 If I Could Read One Book . . .

on prayer with Scripture:
Too Deep for Words: Rediscovering Lectio Divina,
by Thelma Hall

on guided meditation for healing memories:
Prayer, Stress and Our Inner Wounds,
by Flora Slosson Wuellner

Heart of Healing, Heart of Light: Encountering God, Who Shares and Heals Our Pain,
by Flora Slosson Wuellner

on contemplative silence:
Sharing Silence: Meditation Practices and Mindful Living,
by Gunilla Brodde Norris

on seeking spiritual guidance:
Finding a Spiritual Friend: How Friends and Mentors Can Make Your Faith Grow,
by Timothy Jones

Moving On

"Moving beyond your parents' divorce is part of what is necessary to prepare for the fact that its effects will nevertheless continue to be felt."[1]

—Ross A. Thompson

"The process of improvisation that goes into composing a life is compounded in the process of remembering a life, like a patchwork quilt in a watercolor painting, rumpled and evocative. Yet it is in the second process, composing a life through memory as well as through day-to-day choices, that seems to me the most essential to creative living. The past empowers the present, and the groping footsteps leading to this present mark the pathways to the future."[2]

—Mary Catherine Bateson

"As a child I learned hard and fast that everything can fall apart; but as an adult I am slowly learning that everything can come together. And perhaps having this hope is the best ending of all."[3]

—Stephanie Staal

---

1. Ross A. Thompson, e-mail to author, April 26, 2004.
2. Mary Catherine Bateson, in "Composing a Life," quoted by Stephanie Staal, *The Love They Lost: Living with the Legacy of Our Parents' Divorce* (New York: Delacorte Press, 2000), p. 246.
3. Stephanie Staal, *The Love They Lost: Living with the Legacy of Our Parents' Divorce* (New York: Delacorte Press, 2000), p. 246.

Shaken Foundations

Ross Thompson offers the reminder that divorce is a process. It is a process that began before the legal dissolution of your parents' marriage. It is a process that will continue to have a ripple effect on your life long into the future. Part of moving on with your life is to accept this reality and to integrate it into your awareness of the present and your plans for the future. In this last section, we encourage you to think about the following things as you prepare to move on with your life into the open future that awaits your decisions and design.

Honor the Time of "Now"

Take time, make time, beyond all the demands of daily living to be in conversation with yourself about where you are in this moment in regard to your parents' divorce. Clear the space you need to deal with the issues of their divorce so that you are able to make choices about your own life and relationships that seek not to repeat their history.

Do the hard work of grieving and letting go, of envisioning a positive future and acting toward it.

- Assess what you have lost and what you have learned.
- Get to know your parents as individuals. If possible, learn who they are through your adult eyes. Seek to understand who they are as people, not just as parents.
- Look at your own relationships. With courage, make a careful assessment of your patterns in choosing friends and romantic relationships.
- Work on relationships with siblings and other family members. They can be important and valuable resources in providing broader perspectives and additional information about your family's life and your parents' relationship.
- Enlist the help of friends. Discover, affirm, and trust the power of community.
- Seek professional help. Discover the power of this particular kind of companionship for your life journey.
- Deepen your own spiritual life. In dealing with your parents' divorce; recognizing their own vulnerabilities; acknowledging your own pain; pursuing hope, joy, peace, and love in your life; and asking questions that start with "why" you will be led into spiritual territory where the meaning of life is pondered. Consider this an opportunity! Consider this a door that opens for you and invites you to live your life more fully, more freely, more gracefully, more gratefully, more richly, more "really."

You Are Not Your Parents

If you remember only one thing from this book, remember this: *You are not your parents.* They each have their own life stories. They shared a life story for a period of time, short or long. You are part of their life story. They are part of your life story. Their life stories, individually and as your parents, affect your life story but do not determine it. You have the ability to design your life and your relationships differently than theirs.

Your life work is to write your own story. Your life is a gift from God. God intends freedom and fullness of life for all God's people. God intends that people will both be loved and love others as part of God's design for life in community. God intends for love to flow to us and through us, for love to be an abundant resource of creative energy for our lives as we discover and use the gifts we have been given. You have the power to decide how you will live, what you will do with the gift of life you have been given, and how you will relate to yourself, to others, and to God.

Ritualize Your Moving On

You may come to the end of this book and find that it has raised more questions than it has given answers. You may feel that you are only beginning the journey of dealing with your parents' divorce.

On the other hand, you may come to the end of this book feeling as if you have been in good and deep dialogue with it, that it has helped you let go of some things and decide to do others. You may feel that you are ready for the next step in the process of dealing with your parents' divorce.

Remember that your parents' divorce was a process. Coming to understand and deal with that event in your life is a process. Even if you feel ready to move on, you may find yourself coming back sometime in the future with new questions or another layer of wondering about an old question. Significant life events like your own wedding or the birth of a child or the death of one of your parents will open up old feelings. You may encounter some of the material you have dealt with here again and again. However, you may find that each time, the work is different. The view from another stage in life is not quite the same as it is now. Like climbing a mountain on a spiraling path to the top, the view of where you have been will be different at each level of your climb.

It may be helpful for you to ritualize your moving ahead or moving on from this particular place. Here are some suggestions. Take a whole day or part of a day for yourself — a quiet day of reflection or treating yourself to a favorite activity. It may involve doing something with a sibling or another family member, perhaps sharing what you have learned or the questions you still hold. Perhaps it will be lunch with a friend, a special dinner with a life partner, or a family-oriented activity. Completing one journal and beginning a new one, buying flowers for yourself or a book or something new to wear that reflects the inner newness you feel — any of these may be ways to mark this time and move ahead or move on with your life.

Shaken Foundations

Moving On

✎ For Your Reflection:

What was your most significant learning from reading and interacting with this book?

Did you have a companion as you read this material? With whom did you talk about the material in this book? With whom did you trust your reflections on it?

What is your next step?

What kind of ritual might you consider as a mark of moving on?

RECOMMENDED RESOURCES

Enright, Robert. *Forgiveness Is a Choice: A Step by Step Process for Resolving Anger and Restoring Hope.* Washington, D.C.: American Psychological Association, 2001.

Hall, Thelma. *Too Deep for Words: Rediscovering Lectio Divina.* Mahwah, NJ: Paulist Press, 1988.

Jones, Timothy. *Finding a Spiritual Friend: How Friends and Mentors Can Make Your Faith Grow.* Nashville: Upper Room Books, 1998.

_____. *Journeying in Place.* New York: Bell Tower, 1994.

Keen, Sam. *To Love and Be Loved.* New York: Bantam Books, 1997.

Linn, Dennis, Sheila Fabricant Linn, and Matthew Linn. *Don't Forgive Too Soon: Extending the Two Hands that Heal.* Mahwah, NJ: Paulist Press, 1997.

Norris, Gunilla Brodde. *Sharing Silence: Meditation Practices and Mindful Living.* New York: Bell Tower, 1992.

_____. *Becoming Bread: Embracing the Spiritual in the Everyday.* Mahwah, NJ: Paulist Press, 2003.

Richo, David. *How to Be an Adult: A Handbook on Psychological and Spiritual Integration.* Mahwah, NJ: Paulist Press, 1991.

Smedes, Lewis. *The Art of Forgiving.* Nashville: Moorings, 1996.

Staal, Stephanie. *The Love They Lost: Living with the Legacy of Our Parents' Divorce.* New York: Delacorte Press, 2000.

Wallerstein, Judith, and Sandra Blakeslee. *What About the Kids?: Raising Your Children Before, During, and After Divorce.* New York: Hyperion, 2003.

Weems, Ann. *Psalms of Lament.* Louisville: Westminster John Knox Press, 1995.

Wuellner, Flora Slosson. *Heart of Healing, Heart of Light: Encountering God, Who Shares and Heals Our Pain.* Nashville: Upper Room Books, 1992.

Weullner, Flora Slosson. *Prayer, Stress and Our Inner Wounds.* Nashville: Upper Room Books, 1985.

BIBLIOGRAPHY

Dana, Gregg. "Forgiveness," in *Growing*, January 2003, pp. 1–2.

Emery, Robert. "Postdivorce Family Life for Children." Ross A. Thompson and Paul A. Amato, eds. *The Postdivorce Family: Children, Parenting, and Society*. Thousand Oaks, CA: Sage Publications, Inc., 1999.

Lansky, Vicki. *Divorce Book for Parents: Helping Your Children Cope with Divorce and Its Aftermath*. New York: New American Library, 1989.

Levine, Beth. *Divorce: Young People Caught in the Middle*. Springfield, NJ: Enslow Publishers, 1995.

Morton, Nelle. *The Journey Is Home*. Boston: Beacon Press, 1985.

Richo, David. *How to Be an Adult: A Handbook on Psychological and Spiritual Integration*. Mahwah, NJ: Paulist Press, 1991.

Rilke, Ranier Maria. *Letters to a Young Poet*. Translated by Joan M. Burnham. Novato, CA: New World Library, 2000.

Staal, Stephanie. *The Love They Lost: Living with the Legacy of Our Parents' Divorce*. New York: Delacorte Press, 2000.

Thompson, Ross A., and Paul R. Amato. "The Postdivorce Family: An Introduction to the Issues." Ross A. Thompson and Paul A. Amato, eds. *The Postdivorce Family: Children, Parenting, and Society*. Thousand Oaks, CA: Sage Publications, Inc., 1999.

Tripp, Alan. "To Forgive Is More Than Divine," in *Church of the Brethren Messenger*, July 2003, pp. 14–17.

Wallerstein, Judith, and Sandra Blakeslee. *What About the Kids?: Raising Your Children Before, During, and After Divorce*. New York: Hyperion, 2003.

Wallerstein, Judith, Julia Lewis, and Sandra Blakeslee. *The Unexpected Legacy of Divorce: A 25 Year Landmark Study*. New York: Hyperion, 2000.